HIKING TRAILS

SLOW TRAVEL EUROPE

HIKING TRAILS

THE MOST BEAUTIFUL LONG-DISTANCE HIKES
IN 18 EUROPEAN COUNTRIES

ELMAR TEEGELBECKERS

(m)

CONTENTS

01	Lofoten Crossing - Norway	15
02	West Highland Way - Scotland	31
03	Coast to Coast Walk - England	43
04	Skaneleden - Sweden	57
05	Camøno Trail - Denmark	69
06	Dutch Mountain Trail - The Netherlands	81
07	Entre Lesse et Lomme - Belgium	93
08	Mullerthal Trail - Luxembourg	105
09	Main Beskid Trail - Poland	117
10	Schluchtensteig - Germany	129
11	Via Alpina 1 - Switzerland	141
12	GR5 Savoie Mont Blanc - France	155
13	Liechtenstein Trail - Liechtenstein	169
14	Dolomites UNESCO Geotrail - Italy	181
15	Alpe Adria Trail - Austria	197
16	Slovenian Mountain Trail - Slovenia	211
17	GR121 Talaia Ibilbidea - Spain	229
18	Fishermen's Trail - Portugal	239

FOREWORD

The magic of long-distance hiking

Ten years ago, I found myself in Nepal with an old 80-litre backpack. It was hot, it was raining, and I was alone. I was also completely lost. With 44 pounds (20 kilos) on my back and no real plan, I set off on a 125-mile (200 km) trek through the Annapurna Mountains. Along the way, I met other hikers and started walking with them, gradually shedding more of my gear at each guesthouse we stayed in. Most of it, unsurprisingly, was unnecessary. After days of blisters, some hard lessons, and a few tears, I reached the end of the trail, with one thing abundantly clear. I had fallen in love with long-distance hiking.

What I didn't realise then was that you don't need to travel far to find great trails. They're often closer than you think, and as varied as Europe itself. Bit by bit, I began exploring what lay just beyond my doorstep. I walked from coast to coast and across mountain ranges, climbed to huts at 10,000 feet (3000 m), followed fjords and pilgrim paths, and passed through forests, villages, and valleys I'd never heard of. I slept in tents, mountain shelters, hostels, hotels – and now and then, in the homes of strangers. Some trails took three days; the toughest lasted forty. Most fell somewhere in between. Whether it was a wide gravel track or a narrow ridge, Europe's trails never failed to deliver.

With every journey, I was struck by how much the landscapes and cultures changed, and yet how naturally they seemed to blend into one another. Borders might be marked by a stone here or an old barbed wire fence there, but more often than not, there's nothing at all. Europe feels connected. It feels whole. And to me, that's how it should be. Today, this network of trails still links people, regions, and countries, just as it did centuries ago when merchants used them to carry their wares.

This book brings together 2,175 miles (3500 km) of walking routes across 18 countries in Europe. I've walked them all, sometimes solo, often with my friend Jochem, a photographer. One trail, through Poland's Beskid Mountains, is described by my friend and fellow solo hiker, Shanna.

TRAVEL SLOW, THEN A LITTLE SLOWER

Eat, hike, sleep: that's the hiker's mantra. For days, weeks, sometimes even months, that rhythm takes over. How do I get from A to B? Do I have enough food and water? One last glance at the map or GPX track, and off you go. Life becomes simple again. You spend your days outdoors, moving constantly. The rush of everyday life fades – no constant messages, no endless scrolling – and you return to something quieter. It sounds idyllic, and often it is. But make no mistake: hiking can be tough. It's physically demanding, and your body will complain as you climb, descend, and carry your pack for hours on end.

But it's the mental side that's often harder. You can get lonely, homesick, or stuck in your own head. Those moments test you, and you might even consider giving up. But if you keep going, something changes. You get stronger. That's the magic of long-distance hiking. The pain fades. The memories, the friendships, the sense of achievement – those are what stay with you. And chances are, you'll want more. There's something about the trail that just gets under your skin.

TRAIL MAGIC

If there's one thing you can always count on, it's trail magic (an idea that comes from the US, but that's just as alive in Europe). It's those unexpected moments that lift your spirits right when you need it most. Maybe it's something small, like a stranger handing you a cold drink after a long, grueling day. Or something bigger, like the time someone offered me a place to sleep when I found the mountain hut closed. These moments give you a boost. They help you through the toughest stretches and remind you that even on the most remote trails, you're never truly alone.

I hope this book inspires you to set out on a long-distance hike, whether it's your first or one of many. However far you go, you'll discover Europe at its most beautiful on foot, one step at a time.

Happy trails!

Follow our adventures on Instagram @_hiking_trails and find all the trails from this book, including GPX files, on hiking-trails.com.

01 NORWAY

LOFOTEN CROSSING

Trekking above the Arctic Circle

The Long Crossing of the Lofoten Islands is the only unofficial hiking trail in this book. Created by a couple of keen hikers, it links the best routes of the Lofoten (pronounced Loff-ooten) Islands into a true thru-hike from west to east. Crossing the archipelago's four largest islands, all north of the Arctic Circle, the route takes you through rugged, remote terrain. At times, you'll need to hop on a ferry to reach the next island, sailing through the fjords of northern Norway.

99 MILES (160 KM) | 8 STAGES | STRENUOUS | 21,900 FEET (6680 M)↑

The Lofoten Islands stretch for around 110 miles (180 km) north of the Arctic Circle in the Norwegian Sea. The landscape is dramatic – steep peaks rising straight from the sea, deep fjords, white-sand beaches, green valleys and old fishing villages. The four main islands are Austvågøya, Vestvågøya, Flakstadøya and Moskenesøya, and they're surrounded by dozens of smaller ones. Lofoten has a rich fishing heritage dating back to Viking times. Cod is still dried on wooden racks here, and traditional fishing remains a vital part of local life.

Hiking in these parts feels a world away from the well-marked trails of the Alps. The paths are often rocky and unmarked. Every now and then a red dot of paint offers some reassurance. Navigation is mostly digital, using GPX routes and hiking apps. Thanks to Norway's *allemannsretten*, the right to roam, wild camping is allowed, meaning you can wake up in some of the most beautiful places imaginable.

I decide to walk the trail with a few friends and after some planning, the four of us head north to Lofoten. We're camping, and shops are few and far between, so packing takes some thought. We carry freeze-dried meals for breakfast and dinner, plus snacks and fruit to get us through the first stretch. Rain gear sits on top: the weather up here can get pretty rough.

We travel by boat from the coastal town of Bodø, passing small islands scattered across the Vestfjorden. The ferry drops us in Svolvær, the gateway to Austvågøya, the largest and easternmost island of the archipelago, where a taxi takes us to the Matmora trailhead, where we'll begin hiking the next morning.

From sea level, we climb straight into the forest. With a full pack of food, water and camping gear, the adjustment is tough – mine weighs well over 22 pounds (10 kilos). Step by step, we rise above the tree line. The sea slowly comes into view, with mountain peaks all around. Matmora, our first summit, looms ahead. The trail winds along the mountainside and over boulders. It's a promising start.

Weather in Lofoten can change quickly, and we get a taste of it straight away. As the locals say, you get four seasons in a day. One moment it's sunny, the next we're walking through rain and hail, then sun again. We find shelter, change into dry clothes and warm up with some hot pasta bolognese in the tent. After a full day on the move, it tastes amazing.

The next morning the sun is back, and we press on through the mountains. The path hugs a steep ridge as we pass Svolvær, then climbs sharply again. A large steel pipe runs alongside the trail, carrying fresh water from a lake above. In the steepest sections, ropes offer extra grip – weathered but helpful. At the top we reach a small mountain hut, basic but welcoming, with just a bunk bed and a table. It's already taken, so we carry on a little further and put our tents up nearby.

The weather turns again the following day. We've planned a tight itinerary, but the rain makes the trail too dangerous to continue. We cover only a few miles before stopping in Leknes and booking an Airbnb. The delay means we'll have to cover 25 miles (40 km) the next day to stay on track.

Moments like this are a good reminder that it's always wise to build a buffer day or two into your itineraries. We learned our lesson the hard way.

The next stretch winds along fjords until we reach the village of Nusfjord, one of Norway's oldest fishing villages, with traditional red and yellow wooden houses on stilts. Fishing, especially for cod, is still an active industry here. Tourism also plays a growing role, and you can even stay in a typical fisherman's cabin. After more than ten hours (!), we reach Fredvang Bridge, exhausted but exhilarated. This sleek white structure is surrounded by the soaring mountains of Lofoten, and we're treated to a spectacular red and orange sunset. The sight lifts our spirits. It's nearly midnight by the time we set up camp and heat up some food, but the light lingers. In summer, it never gets fully dark.

After a deep sleep, we continue towards Kvalvika Beach, one of the highlights of the trip and of the whole archipelago. It looks almost tropical, with turquoise water and white sand, though the air is crisp and the setting framed by fjords and sharp ridges. It's a bit busier here, popular with tourists. From the beach, the trail climbs again, and we cross another pass with wide views across the coastline. The scenery never gets old.

On day six, we catch a ferry to the last island, Moskenesøya, and ask the captain to drop us off in Forsfjorden Bay. Even the boat ride through the fjords is an experience in itself, and we prepare for the day ahead. Today we're climbing Hermannsdalstinden, the highest peak in Lofoten. Since we plan on returning the same way, we leave our heavy packs at the bottom and begin the steep, technical climb. Ropes and chains help in the trickier parts, and eventually we reach the summit at over 3,200 feet (1000 m). The 360-degree view is astonishing: fjords, peaks, villages and sea stretching in every direction. I even manage a quick power nap at the top, soaking in the silence.

Our final two days take us to the western edge of the crossing, Stokkvika. We first stop in Moskenes, where we finally get to shower at a campsite. It feels brilliant to wash off the grime. That evening, we reward ourselves with fish burgers at the café, a huge upgrade after days of freeze-dried food.

On the final day, we cross one last mountain pass, descend one final slope and follow the trail as it hugs the cliffs above the sea. We pitch our tent for the last night in this wild Norwegian landscape. Boiling water for one more meal, we opt for cowboy camping: sleeping under the open sky, no tent, just a mat and sleeping bag. There's something incredibly liberating about it. The sunset is glorious, and a quiet satisfaction creeps over us as we watch the light fade and say goodbye to the trail.

01 NORWAY
LOFOTEN CROSSING

Know before you go
The Long Crossing of the Lofoten Islands isn't an official trail but a tough route linking several hiking paths. It crosses steep ridge lines and rugged alpine terrain. Attempt it only if you're an experienced mountain hiker with confidence in exposed and remote terrain.

PRACTICAL INFO

Country: Norway
Start and end point: Matmora to Stokkvika
Distance: 99 miles (160 km)
Duration: 7-11 days
Difficulty: Strenuous
Best time to go: June to September
Terrain: Mountains, coast, fjords
Elevation gain: 21,900 feet (6680 m)

Our suggested stages
- Matmora trailhead to Botnvated | 12 miles (20 km)
- Botnvated to Olderfjorden | 15 miles (25 km)
- Olderfjorden to Kringbotsnavet | 14 miles (22 km)
- Kringbotsnavet to Leknes | 6 miles (10 km)
- Leknes to Fredvang camp | 25 miles (40 km)
- Fredvang camp to Fageråvatnet | 11 miles (18 km)
- Fageråvatnet to Moskenes | 14 miles (23 km)
- Moskenes to Stokkvika | 11 miles (18 km)

Wild camping is allowed here, so you can walk as much or as little as you like each day. There's no need to stick to a set schedule, so let the weather and your own pace decide the distance. After reaching the endpoint at Stokkvika, just follow the trail back a short way to return to civilisation.

Highlights
- Climbing Hermannsdalstinden, Lofoten's highest peak
- Wandering along the golden sands of Kvalvika Beach
- Eating *kanelboller*, Norwegian cinnamon buns
- Taking the ferry across the fjords to Fjordfjorden

Sleep and shelter
Norway's *allemannsretten* (right to roam) allows you to wild camp almost anywhere. Take full advantage of good weather days, and don't hesitate to slow down when conditions turn. The terrain can become slippery and hazardous in rain.

MORE MULTI-DAY HIKES IN NORWAY

Jotunheimen Traverse | 58 miles (94 km)
Walk along ridges and valleys in Jotunheimen National Park. Sleep in a tent with fjord views or stay in a mountain hut.

Finnskogleden Trail | 150 miles (240 km)
Follow the quiet trails of Finnish immigrants from the 1600s along the Sweden-Norway border. Remote, peaceful, and steeped in history.

St. Olavsleden | 260 miles (580 km)
Often called "the Camino of the North," this pilgrimage trail spans from Sweden's Baltic Sea coast to Norway, ending in Tromsø. Walk in the footsteps of King Olav Haraldsson.

02 SCOTLAND

WEST HIGHLAND WAY

Lochside walking in the Scottish Highlands

The West Highland Way is one of Europe's most popular long-distance walks, and for good reason. This five to seven-day trail weaves through glens, past lochs, and through a dramatic Highland landscape, offering something for beginners and seasoned hikers alike. Along the way, you'll tackle the Devil's Staircase, wild camp in some of the most breathtaking spots (or opt for a cosy local hotel), and often find yourself swapping stories with fellow walkers and locals over a pint in a pub.

96 MILES (154 KM) | 7 STAGES | MODERATE | 9,842 FEET (3000 M)↑

When I told some friends I was planning to walk the West Highland Way, they jumped at the opportunity to join me. Surprisingly, they wanted to go all in, wild camping included. It was their first long-distance hike, but I must've painted an appealing picture. We start in Milngavie, just a short train ride from Glasgow, at the official starting point (marked by a stone pillar), and after stocking up at the supermarket, we take a quick photo and set off.

Heavily loaded, we make our way through the village and out into the countryside. Along the path, honesty boxes with drinks and snacks (which you pay for by leaving money in a postbox) tempt us. Maybe we didn't need to carry quite so much after all? The trail takes us past a local whisky distillery, and when the rain starts, we take shelter at the Beech Tree Inn, the first of many welcoming pubs we'll visit along the way.

Finding a spot to pitch our tents on the first night takes a bit of trial and error. In Scotland, wild camping is generally allowed – just not on farmland, near houses or roads, or in protected nature reserves. Eventually, we settle on a quiet spot in the woods, heat up some freeze-dried meals, and crawl into our sleeping bags.

The next day, we tackle a steep climb up Conic Hill. It's a brilliant place to camp, if you can manage the 19-mile (almost 30 km) trek to get there.

The landscape feels quintessentially Scottish: barren hills, wandering sheep, a lone leafless tree. From the summit, we gaze down over Loch Lomond, nearly 700 feet (200 m) deep, carved by glaciers during the last ice age. After descending, we follow the lake's eastern shore, take a dip in its icy waters, then camp near the hostel in Rowardennan, where we shower and grab a beer from the Loch Lomond Brewery.

Day three brings the toughest stretch: a long, technical path along the loch through sparse, misty forest. It's pouring and the rocks are slippery underfoot. We're constantly climbing up and down, making slow progress. It's hard going, but it's beautiful. We decide to stop, like many others, at the Inversnaid Hotel, and it's the perfect mid-hike pick-me-up. It gives us the boost we need, and before long, with Loch Lomond behind us, we reach Beinglas Campsite where we reward ourselves with a well-earned pint and toast to surviving the long day.

Day four is our longest: over 19 miles (almost 30 km) to Bridge of Orchy. It feels even longer after nights of broken sleep and aching shoulders. Luckily, the trail starts to follow easier gravel paths, and we finally settle into the rhythm of carrying our packs. Midway, we pause at a supermarket to restock before pushing through the final miles.

When we reach the old stone bridge after nine hours on foot, I see the relief on my friends' faces. Secretly, I'm glad to have made it too. It's a stunning spot to wild camp, right beside the historic Bridge of Orchy. River views, a setting sun, and the sound of cascading water from Loch Tulla. We cook dinner at a picnic table and swap stories from the day. These are the moments I hike for: not just the views, but the shared effort and wonder. You have to experience it to understand. It's like a runner's high; you don't know it until you feel it.

From the bridge, the trail leads us deeper into the Highlands. With our hiking legs now properly broken in, we start to enjoy the miles more. The brown peaks of Glencoe rise ahead, and soon we're zigzagging up the Devil's Staircase, a path built in the 18th century by soldiers hauling heavy equipment. The name makes it sound worse than it is, and despite our packs, the climb isn't too bad. At the top, we pause to take in the view of the Munros, Scotland's mighty 3,000-footers (914 m). This is the highest point on the trail, at 1,800 feet (548 m), and we take a well-deserved break before the long descent into Kinlochleven, our final campsite.

The last day sees us walking over quiet hills and gravel roads towards Fort William. In the distance, Ben Nevis comes into view. The town itself is full of pubs and gear shops, a hub for hikers. We meet others who, like us, are finishing the West Highland Way today. Finally, we end at the statue of a tired walker, nicknamed "Sore Feet," and give each other a hug. We've done it: crossed the Highlands, carried everything we needed, and camped along the way. That night, we treat ourselves to a hotel. The bed feels like heaven.

Fort William might be the end of this trail, but it's also the start of another. From here, you can take on the Great Glen Way or even tackle Ben Nevis. At 4,413 feet (1345 m), it's not easy. Expect snow and rugged terrain. But if the West Highland Way teaches you anything, it's that you're capable of more than you think.

02 SCOTLAND
WEST HIGHLAND WAY

Know before you go

The West Highland Way is a challenging yet accessible introduction to long-distance hiking. Thanks to the many restaurants and small shops along the trail, you won't need to carry much food. You can camp at designated campsites or try wild camping, which is legal in much of Scotland and a great way to ease into backpacking. If you prefer more comfort, you'll also find hotels and B&Bs along the way, like we did: mixing camping with a few nights in a bed (and a hot shower).

PRACTICAL INFO
Country: Scotland
Start and end point: Milngavie to Fort William
Distance: 96 miles (154 km)
Duration: 5-7 days
Difficulty: Moderate
Best time to go: May to September
Terrain: Mountains, hills, forest
Elevation gain: 9,842 feet (3000 m)

Our suggested stages
- Milngavie to Conic Hill | 19 miles (30 km)
- Conic Hill to Rowardennan | 11 miles (18 km)
- Rowardennan to Beinglas | 13 miles (21 km)
- Beinglas to Bridge of Orchy | 19 miles (30 km)
- Bridge of Orchy to Glencoe | 11 miles (18 km)
- Glencoe to Kinlochleven | 11 miles (18 km)
- Kinlochleven to Fort William | 15 miles (25 km)

You can walk the West Highland Way in five or six stages, depending on your pace. Suggested itineraries are available at hiking-trails.com/trail/west-highland-way.

Highlights
- Wild camping in the Scottish Highlands
- Climbing the Devil's Staircase
- Taking a dip in Loch Lomond
- Local beers and pub grub

Sleep and shelter
You can sleep at campsites near the villages or wild camp along the trail. Many hikers mix both options. Villages also offer hotels and B&Bs, but availability is limited, so be sure to book early.

MORE MULTI-DAY HIKES IN SCOTLAND

Great Glen Way | 78 miles (125 km)
The Great Glen Way starts where the West Highland Way ends. It takes you coast to coast past lochs like Loch Ness, ending in Inverness, the capital of the Highlands.

Skye Trail | 80 miles (128 km)
A rugged hike across the Isle of Skye, Scotland's largest island. Known as the "Isle of Mist," the trail features windswept cliffs and the iconic Old Man of Storr.

Speyside Way | 85 miles (137 km)
Easy walking along well-marked trails through Scotland's whisky country. Follow the River Spey past distilleries and old rail lines on this relaxed but scenic trail.

03 ENGLAND

COAST TO COAST WALK

From sea to sea through rural England

Follow in the footsteps of Alfred Wainwright, British fell walker, writer, and illustrator, on the iconic Coast to Coast Walk. This route, one of the UK's designated National Trails, stretches from the west to the east coast of England, crossing three national parks. En route, you'll pass through rural villages where you can stay at a charming B&B or put up your tent in a pub garden and recover with some fish and chips and a pint. The trail is demanding in places, particularly in the Lake District, but the beauty of the English countryside makes every step worth it.

195 MILES (313 KM) | 12 STAGES | DIFFICULT | 29,035 FEET (8850 M)↑

Our journey begins in St Bees, on England's northwest coast. Following tradition, we dip a toe into the Irish Sea to mark the start of our adventure, vowing to do the same in the North Sea at the journey's end. Then we set off, beginning with a scenic coastal stretch that attracts birdwatchers from around the world. This is the only place in England where guillemots breed on the rugged cliffs.

Our trail leads us inland to Ennerdale Bridge, and few hikes begin as promisingly. Leaving the wild coast behind, we enter the Lake District, the first and arguably most rugged of the national parks we'll pass through. We wrap up our first day in picturesque Ennerdale where we stay at the Fox and Hounds Inn and are quickly introduced to local pub life.

Hikers and locals come and go, creating a communal atmosphere. We chat with two Australian walkers – one, aged 70, tells us it's been her lifelong dream to walk this trail and she's delighted to have completed day one. At this pub, as with many others along the trail, you can pitch your tent in the beer garden for just £10. You'll often find showers available, and the food is hearty and satisfying. We set our tent up and are soon joined by two more hikers who become familiar faces in the days to come. For now, we're exhausted and retreat early to our sleeping bags.

The first four days through the Lake District are breathtaking, but the constant ascents and descents over rolling hills make it one of the toughest parts of the Coast to Coast Walk. Here, the trail offers two options: the high route over mountain ridges, or the easier low route through valleys and villages. We choose the high route and our calves pay the price. I now understand the true meaning of "scrambling" as we clamber over rocks, grateful for the dry weather. Though the highest point is just 2,641 (850 m) feet, with heavy packs it feels like an alpine challenge.

After three long days, we reach Kidsty Pike, the most iconic peak in the area, with sweeping views of lakes and mountains. We finish the day in Shap and join the long queue outside the famous Shap Chippy (ranked the second-best fish and chip shop in the UK) for a well-earned treat.

Next, we enter the Yorkshire Dales, the second national park on our route. After the Lake District, the softer, greener hills feel like a welcome reprieve. We meet Tom, a park ranger responsible for maintaining trails and signage. Since the route crosses private farmland, rangers install and maintain hundreds of gates to ensure cattle stay contained. Not long after our chat, we see Tom again, drill in hand, repairing a fence while trying to catch escaped horses. It's a reminder of the quiet work that keeps these trails alive.

After six days, we reach Keld, a tiny village where we pitch our tent beside the river. A supply package we sent ahead awaits us: freeze-dried meals we didn't want to carry from the start. While we often eat in pubs, we also prepare simple meals by our tent (though a pub snack still sneaks in most nights). Grateful for a moment of sunshine, we reorganise our gear before heading to the local pub for a drink. There, we chat with two Englishmen

in their fifties who've travelled the world but still believe that nothing beats the English countryside. Impressed by our decision to discover "their" Coast to Coast Walk, they treat us to a drink and toast our adventure. Eventually, we bid our goodbyes and prepare for the second part of the trail.

The next day, we walk from Keld to Reeth, perhaps one of the trail's most beautiful stretches. We see no one else as we wind through yellow-green hills dotted with medieval ruins and stone bridges before finally arriving in Reeth, nestled in one of Yorkshire's many dales and enclosed by low stone walls.

Stages eight and nine, from Reeth to Ingleby Cross, are flatter and less scenic. At times, the gravel paths and lack of views test our patience.

But soon, the third and final national park – the North York Moors – more than makes up for it. This vast moorland is home to flocks of curlews that seem to follow us from valley to valley. The trail winds through more achingly beautiful English countryside, and we soak in the views. During this stretch, we often hike with Ian and Graham, a father-and-son-in-law duo from Newcastle we first met on day one. We keep our own paces but reconnect in the evenings to eat together and chat. You form a kind of friendship with strangers when hiking. It's one of the most special things about the whole experience for me.

As we pass through the North York Moors, we stop at the Lion Inn in Blakey Ridge for a coffee. This 16th-century pub stands at the park's highest

point, overlooking the valleys. Inside, red carpets, wooden furniture, and stone walls give it an old-world charm. A perfect place for an overnight stay.

Twelve days in, we spot the North Sea on the horizon; Robin Hood's Bay, our destination, lies just ahead. On Spring Bank Holiday, the village is buzzing with people. After crossing the country, we dip our toes in the sea once more, before finally reaching Wainwright's Bar, the official end of the Coast to Coast Walk, where we see the sign marking our finish. The pub is full, but a man notices our weary joy and buys us a beer. We toast the end of an unforgettable journey: coast to coast through England's rolling hills. Certainly, a trek to remember.

03 ENGLAND
COAST TO COAST WALK

National Trails
The UK has a fantastic network of long-distance walking routes. England and Wales are home to 17 National Trails, while Scotland has its own set of Great Trails. The Coast to Coast Walk, one of the country's best-loved hikes, was officially added to the National Trails list in 2022 after a successful petition by British walkers.

Know before you go
The best time to explore the area is in spring or early autumn (May to September), when the crowds are smaller. Accommodation can be limited in small villages, so it's wise to book B&Bs in advance. If you're camping, there are plenty of campgrounds available, and many pubs even offer space for tents. Be prepared for rain, so bring appropriate rain gear. In the Lake District, wet rocks can be especially slippery, so exercise caution. If the weather conditions are poor, it's safer to take the low route.

PRACTICAL INFO

Country: England
Start and end point: St. Bees to Robin Hood's Bay
Distance: 195 miles (313 km)
Duration: 12 days
Difficulty: Difficult
Best time to go: May to September
Terrain: Hills, coast, countryside
Elevation gain: 29,035 feet (8850 m)

Our suggested stages
- St Bees to Ennerdale Bridge | 14 miles (23 km)
- Ennerdale Bridge to Borrowdale | 14 miles (23 km)
- Borrowdale to Patterdale | 15 miles (25 km)
- Stage 4: Patterdale to Shap | 15 miles (25 km)
- Stage 5: Shap to Kirkby Stephen | 19 miles (31 km)
- Kirkby Stephen to Keld | 12 miles (19 km)
- Keld to Reeth | 11 miles (18 km)
- Reeth to Brompton-on-Swale | 16 miles (26 km)
- Brompton-on-Swale to Ingleby Cross | 17 miles (28 km)
- Ingleby Cross to Blakey Ridge | 10 miles (16 km)
- Blakey Ridge to Littlebeck | 17 miles (28 km)
- Littlebeck to Robin Hood's Bay | 19 miles (31 km)

Highlights
- The views from Kidsty Pike
- Fish & chips at Shap Chippy
- Overnight stay at Kirkby Stephen Church Hostel
- A pint at Wainwright's Bar in Robin Hood's Bay

Sleep and shelter
Overnight options along the trail include pubs, B&Bs, youth hostels, and campgrounds. In many cases, you can also put your tent up in pub gardens. If you plan to stay in a pub or B&B, it's important to book in advance, as space can be limited. Youth hostels and campgrounds, on the other hand, typically have availability, so you're more likely to find a spot without a reservation.

MORE MULTI-DAY HIKES IN ENGLAND

South West Coast Path | 630 miles (1014 km)
The longest marked trail in England, tracing the coast of Somerset, Devon, Cornwall, and Dorset.

Pennine Way | 268 miles (431 km)
A tough route along the Pennines, with rugged moorlands and remote beauty.

Hadrian's Wall Path | 184 miles (135 km)
This trail, which also runs coast to coast, offers a more leisurely and slightly shorter alternative to the Coast to Coast route, following the path of Hadrian's Wall.

 SWEDEN

SKÅNELEDEN

Into the woods of southern Sweden

Down in Skåne, the southernmost part of Sweden, there are over 800 miles (1300 km) of hiking trails waiting to be explored. The Skåneleden trail network consists of six routes that criss-cross the region, winding through forests and fields, skirting rock formations, and tracing the coastline. It's not a challenging trail, but the ever-changing landscape is what makes it truly enjoyable.

62 MILES (100 KM) | 4 STAGES | EASY | 4,921 FEET (1500 M)↑

We walked a section of Skåneleden 2 (SL2 – Nord till Syd), which stretches from Hårsjö in the north to the coastal town of Trelleborg in the south. From this long route, we picked four stages between Vittsjö and Höör (about 62 miles, or 100 km, in total) which we covered over four days.

The trail is also a fantastic spot for birdwatching. Skåne sits right on one of Europe's busiest migratory paths, with around 500 million birds passing through each year. So while you're out on the trail, keep an eye out for kestrels, buzzards, and red kites.

We began our hike at the campsite in Vittsjö, right by Lake Vittsjön. Back in Viking times, when Denmark was larger and more powerful than it is today, this town lay on the border between Sweden and Denmark and held great strategic importance. Today, it's a key junction thanks to the *Markarydsbanan* railway running just beyond it. It's a convenient starting point, as the trail leads straight from the campsite into the forest. Heading north toward Hårsjö, we cross a road that once served as a main route for Danish partisans in around 1600, on their way to Hovdala Castle nearby. Back then, this border region was tense, and an enemy could appear from the woods at any moment. Now, the path is peaceful, as if none of that ever happened. We count ourselves lucky.

Following the meandering Hörlingeån River, we make our way to a small lake where we pitch our tent after about 17 miles (30 km). It's a beautiful

spring day, though the evening turns chilly, so we pull on our down jackets before sunset. We heat water on our gas burner and prepare a freeze-dried meal. Tonight's menu: spaghetti bolognese. It might sound unlikely, but after a long day of hiking, it tastes almost restaurant-worthy.

One of the best things about Sweden is the freedom to camp, thanks to *allemansrätten*, a unique Scandinavian tradition that gives everyone the right to access nature and the outdoors. It's all about respecting that nature is something we share. Of course, there are some simple rules to follow: don't leave any rubbish or traces behind, and always keep a good distance from homes and farmland.

The next day, we head north through dense forest, choosing to walk around Lake Finjasjön to avoid the urban area on the left. We wanted to stay in nature as much as possible, though you could easily take the other route and even spend the night near the lake in Hässleholm. The trail winds along wooden boardwalks through thick vegetation, with occasional glimpses of the water where anglers fish for perch. At a small sandy beach, we spot an abandoned canoe and pause to take in the view. The only sounds are birds calling through the trees. It's utterly peaceful.

The path winds through the Göingeåsen Nature Reserve on the way to Hovdala. Every so often, we pass a Swedish house painted in bright yellow or red, tucked away in the middle of the forest. Eventually, we reach Hovdala Slott in Hässleholm. With its tall white tower and arched entrance, the 16th-century castle stands out against the surrounding woods. Once a stronghold during the 17th-century wars between Sweden and Denmark, it's been destroyed and rebuilt several times but remains one of the region's most iconic landmarks. Its white stone walls and dark red roofs give it a distinctly medieval charm, and after a rest at the nearby café, we continue a bit further to find a quiet place to settle down for the night. Flat ground is scarce, but eventually we come across a small open field deep in the forest.

The final stretch toward Höör is a pleasant one. We pass several shelters that could serve as overnight stops, and the trail eventually widens into a road that leads straight into Höör, where we end our walk at the train station. At last, it's time for *fika*, a beloved Swedish tradition that roughly translates to taking a break to enjoy coffee and cake with good company. We embrace the ritual at Café Old Fashion, a fitting end to our journey. From Höör, we catch the train back to Vittsjö and walk the short path back to the campsite.

The forests of Sweden are a true breath of fresh air. Throughout our long-distance hike, we only encountered a handful of other walkers and while the landscape might not vary wildly, you're constantly immersed in nature and surrounded by woodland. And when you do cross paths with someone, whether a local or a fellow hiker, they're always warm and friendly.

04 SWEDEN
SKÅNELEDEN

Know before you go

The Skåneleden is a long-distance hiking trail that spans 808 miles (1300 km) through Skåne, Sweden's southernmost province. It's divided into six sub-trails with a total of 113 sections, so it's perfect for both day hikes or longer treks. The entire trail is clearly marked with orange signs, making it easy to follow. You can walk along the coast or head inland through central Skåne, where you'll find green beech forests, fascinating rock formations, and rich flora and fauna. The trail also passes dozens of lakes.

PRACTICAL INFO

Country: Sweden
Start and end point: Vittsjö to Höör
Distance: 62 miles (100 km)
Duration: 4 days
Difficulty: Easy
Best time to go: April to October
Terrain: Forest
Elevation gain: 4,921 feet (1500 m)

Our suggested stages
- Vittsjö to Hågnarp | 18 miles (29 km)
- Hågnarp to Finja | 15 miles (24 km)
- Finja to Hovdala | 15 miles (24 km)
- Hovdala to Höör | 20 miles (32 km)

Highlights
- *Fika*, a stop for coffee and cake at a local bakery
- Wild camping in the vast forests
- A visit to the historic Hovdala Slott
- Birdwatching, as Skåne is home to a rich variety of birdlife

Sleep and shelter
Thanks to Sweden's "everyman's right" (*allemansrätten*), you can wild camp along the trail. There are also free shelters, simple wooden huts, scattered along the route. Just bring your own sleeping gear, food, and water. If you prefer more comfort, you'll find B&Bs and guest-houses in villages at the end of many stages.

MORE MULTI-DAY HIKES IN SWEDEN

High Coast Trail | 84 miles (135 km)
Walk this UNESCO World Heritage Site along the Gulf of Bothnia, through beaches, forests, and fishing villages in the Höga Kusten area.

Bohusleden | 217 miles (350 km)
A trail through the forests just north of Gothenburg, where you can stay in simple wooden shelters overnight. You might not see another soul for days.

Kungsleden | 280 miles (450 km)
A true classic among Europe's long-distance hikes. Far in the north, this challenging route runs from Abisko to Nikkaluokta through Arctic landscapes, attracting hikers from around the world.

05 DENMARK

CAMØNO TRAIL

Island hopping in Denmark

We're in southeastern Denmark on the Camøno Trail, or *Camønoen* as the Danes call it. Known as Denmark's friendliest hiking route, it winds across the islands of Møn, Bogø and Nyord, offering a peaceful and scenic alternative to the country's better-known cycle paths. Along the way, we pass pebbly beaches, chalk cliffs and quiet villages – and, if we're lucky, stumble upon 70-million-year-old fossils on the shores of the Møns Klint UNESCO World Heritage Site or stargaze in one of the darkest corners of Europe.

109 MILES (175 KM) | 7 STAGES | EASY | 2,460 FEET (750 M)↑

This 109-mile (175 km) long-distance hike begins on Møn, the largest of the three islands, in the old trading town of Stege. On our way to the starting point, we pass through the old town and see a mix of architecture from different eras. Minimalist modern façades stand beside timber-framed buildings from the 11th century, often painted in cheerful colours. Møn Museum, a traditional building painted in yellow, marks the trail's official starting point. You can even stay the night here on one of the wooden beds in the barn, provided you bring your own sleeping pad and bag.

From here, we follow the well-marked hiking trails towards Nyord. What strikes us first is the stillness, the almost indescribable tranquillity. We are the only ones on the trail, apart from a few men casting their lines from the bridge. Nyord is a tiny island, just 2 square miles (5 square km) in area, of which nearly 80 percent is uninhabitable marshland, regularly flooded by the Baltic Sea at high tide. We climb the observation tower and look out over the wetlands, home to hundreds of bird species. You can spot greenshanks, avocets, lapwings and redshanks – or, with any luck, some bald eagles, ospreys or peregrine falcons.

Our first shelter is in the inhabited part of the island: Hyldevang, a hiking shelter with open wooden huts that sleep around four people and are free to use for hikers and cyclists. You often find several together with a fire pit and, if you're lucky, some firewood. We roll out our sleeping mats and bags for a comfortable night's sleep.

From the shelter, we walk to the harbour and visit the small octagonal church, wandering through the peaceful (and only) village, lined with charming old farmhouses. On a clear night between September and March, you can even see the Milky Way stretching above, thanks to the total absence of light pollution.

Back at the shelter, we build a campfire and prepare our dinner. A pink sunset glows over the horizon as we crawl into our sleeping bags, still warm from the fire, for our first night under the stars.

The trail continues along the coast, back towards Møn. For the first time, we come across a few tourists enjoying a dip in the water on this warm day. Leaving the coast behind and heading inland, we catch sight of the white Elmelunde Church in the distance. Once a landmark for trading ships on the Baltic Sea, the church towers above the landscape. Its whitewashed walls and red roofs make it a beautiful sight. Excavations nearby have uncovered remains from the Bronze Age, long before the current stone structure was built. Today, the church is open to all, and the frescoes on its ceiling are stunning. Only a few steps away is our bed and breakfast. As the sun sets, the white church takes on a warm red glow. It feels magical.

The next day, we continue to the Møns Klint UNESCO World Heritage Site and its famous white chalk cliffs. The miles of coastline, with its dramatic limestone formations and azure water, feel almost tropical. Thanks to the rich soil, a unique selection of plant species grows here, especially vibrant in early summer. Wooden staircases lead down through beech forest to the beaches, where you can walk beneath the cliffs or along them for panoramic views. We wander along the pebbly beach, searching for ancient fossils, and visit the GeoCenter a little inland to learn more about the area's natural history.

We soon push on towards Bogø, the third island. This is the toughest stretch – not because of any hills, but because we're walking over sand. Following the coastline, we reach our next shelter at Slotshaven, just before the bridge to the island. Birds nest in the chalk cliffs above as we settle in for the night. We light a fire and heat up our food while the sun sinks into the sea.

Bogø lies west of Møn and marks the final island on our journey. Long owned by Danish royalty, the island is now connected to Møn by a car bridge without a footpath. We opt to take the bus across, which drops us at Bogø harbour where sailboats bob in the water. From here, you can take a

ferry to the larger island of Falster. This is one of Denmark's oldest wooden ferries and a popular route for cyclists exploring the archipelago.

There's also a culinary gem tucked away here. Christian, an Italian baker, now lives in Bogø and makes some of the best bread and pizza in Denmark. The *kanelsnegl* – a Danish cinnamon roll – is delicious, and we return to BogøBrød in the evening for pizza. As we eat, we watch the last ferry pull away from the dock before settling in for the night in the nearby shelter, satisfied and sleepy.

We prepare for the final two stages of the trail, which take us back to Stege, where we started. The path follows the coastline, and we spend the night at the Mønbroen campsite. From here, we can see the Queen Alexandrine Bridge, which links Møn to Zealand, Denmark's largest island and home to Copenhagen. On our last day, we head inland once more towards Stege.

After 109 miles (175 km), our island-hopping hike draws to a close. Denmark has surprised us, from its wild cliffs and gleaming white churches to its almost tropical beaches and welcoming shelters. We already know we'll return.

05 DENMARK
CAMØNO TRAIL

Know before you go

The Camøno Trail is perfect for hikers who love peace and simplicity. The trail is non-technical and well-marked, though a couple of sandy sections require a bit of endurance. With frequent villages and shelters, it's easy to adjust stages to your pace. Don't miss the detour to the white chalk cliffs of Møns Klint, a UNESCO World Heritage Site.

PRACTICAL INFO

Country: Denmark
Start and end point: Stege
Distance: 109 miles (175 km)
Duration: 7 days
Difficulty: Easy
Best time to go: May to September
Terrain: Coast, urban, countryside
Elevation gain: 2,460 feet (750)

Our suggested stages
- Stege to Nyord | 10 miles (16 km)
- Nyord to Elmehøj | 12 miles (19 km)
- Elmehøj to Møns Klint | 10 miles (16 km)
- Møns Klint to Slotshaven | 22 miles (35 km)
- Slotshaven to Bogø | 15 miles (25 km)
- Bogø to Mønbroen | 15 miles (25 km)
- Mønbroen to Stege | 12 miles (19 km)

The total distance of all the stages adds up to slightly less than the full trail, since you often walk a few extra miles from the trail to the nearby villages on the islands.

Highlights
- Standing next to the white cliffs of Møns Klint
- Tasting *kanelsnegle* at BogøBrød bakery
- Stargazing in Nyord's dark sky area
- Spotting the iconic whitewashed churches of Møn

Sleep and shelter
There are several free shelters along the trail. Just bring a sleeping mat and bag — no tent needed. Most shelters are roomy and operate on a first-come, first-served basis. If one's full, there's usually a guesthouse or campsite not far away.

MORE MULTI-DAY HIKES IN DENMARK

Hærvejen | 311 miles (500 km)
Denmark's longest trail, taking in forest, heathland, farmland, and coast along an old trade route through the heart of the country.

Archipelago Trail | 137 miles (220 km)
A tranquil coastal walk past fishing villages, birdwatching havens, and sea cliffs along southern Fyn's island-studded shoreline.

Mols Bergje Trail | 50 miles (80 km)
This four-stage hike in Denmark's "mountains" (which reach a height of 150 feet) connects the harbour town of Ebeltoft to the ruined Kalø Castle overlooking the bay.

06 THE NETHERLANDS

DUTCH MOUNTAIN TRAIL

Climbing the seven summits of South Limburg

Since 2020, the Netherlands has had a surprisingly challenging long-distance hike, the Dutch Mountain Trail (DMT). Forget flat meadows and polders—this route takes you over hills, valleys, quarries, and even the country's highest point, the Vaalserberg. Over about 60 miles (100 km), the trail crosses seven summits in South Limburg, passing old mines and traces of both World Wars. It's a four-day journey through the "mountains" of Europe's lowest-lying country.

63 MILES (101 KM) | 4 STAGES | EASY | 6,233 FEET (1900 M)↑

The DMT starts at Eygelshoven railway station and ends at Maastricht, right by its station. You can split the walk however you like, but most people take four days, covering 14 to 17 miles (22 to 28 km) each day. Some runners complete it in just over ten hours, but I chose the relaxed four-day pace, perfect for a long weekend. I camped at three sites, each at the end of a stage. But if you prefer more comfort, there are hotels and B&Bs in villages along the way.

The first stage begins at Eygelshoven and ends in Vaals, the Netherlands' most famous mountain village. Vaals sits on the edge of an ancient volcano, with the nearby German city of Aachen lying right in its crater, a fascinating reminder of the earth's forces beneath us. The trail winds through the beautiful Limburg landscape: rolling hills, beech forests, and villages with church spires rising from their centres.

We follow the Miljoenenlijn, an old railway once used to haul coal and soon pass the "dragon's teeth": large triangular concrete blocks from WWII that were part of the 375-mile-long Westwall defence line. From here, we climb our first summit, Wilhelminaberg. A short stretch into Germany brings us to the second peak, Schneeberg, where we enjoy sweeping views over Vaals and its church tower, before descending to Gastmolen campsite, where we set up our tent in the hikers' field.

Our second day takes us through the Netherlands' highest "mountains," from Vaals to Gulpen. This stage feels more alpine, with some serious climbs. First up: the Vaalserberg. At 1,050 feet (322 m), it marks the three-border point between the Netherlands, Belgium, and Germany. After Napoleon's defeat, both Prussia and the Netherlands wanted the area's zinc mines, and when Belgium broke away from the Netherlands in 1830, a small neutral country by the name of Moresnet was formed, creating a temporary four-country point. It existed until WWI, which we were interested to discover. From here, the trail passes through quiet farms and villages, even past vineyards which offer views that feel almost French. Then, after 14 miles (23 km), we finally reach the village of Gulpen.

Day three starts with a lung-busting climb up the Gulperberg, a steep hill popular with Dutch cyclists. From the top, the views stretch wide over the surrounding countryside and the Eyserbos forest. Two more summits await: Hakkenberg, where the borders of the Netherlands, Wallonia, and Flanders meet, and Kattenroth. Along the way, we pass old half-timbered houses and follow roads that once carried grain and coal down to the Meuse River. The trail winds past ruins and quarries, and after six hours of hiking, we reach Mheer, our home for the night.

The last stretch toward Maastricht includes some steep and tricky sections, especially when the trail is muddy, so trekking poles come in handy. Our final "summit," D'n Observant, isn't actually a mountain but rather a waste heap created from local marl mining. Its name comes from a Franciscan monastery that once stood nearby. From its slopes, we look out over the Meuse Valley below.

We then walk down past the vast ENCI limestone quarry and its marl caves. This is also where the famous Pieterpad long-distance trail ends, a beautiful route in its own right. From there, it's an easy stroll along the Maasboulevard straight into Maastricht. After four days and 63 miles (101 km), we reach the train station, tired but satisfied.

06 THE NETHERLANDS
DUTCH MOUNTAIN TRAIL

Know before you go

The area between the Meuse and Rhine rivers, where the lowlands begin to rise into hills, has a rich history. Subsoil deposits date back nearly 300 million years to the Carboniferous period and include chalk formations from around 100 million years ago. These layers helped establish the region's coal mining and marl quarrying industries. Today, the fertile soil is perfect for orchards and vineyards and is home to badgers, beavers, and kingfishers. Many hikers use the DMT as preparation for tougher trails, including the GR5 from the Hook of Holland to Nice.

PRACTICAL INFO

Country: Netherlands
Start and end point: Eygelshoven to Maastricht
Distance: 63 miles (101 km)
Duration: 4 days
Difficulty: Easy
Best time to go: April to October
Terrain: Hills
Elevation gain: 6,233 feet

Our suggested stages
- Eygelshoven Station to Vaals | 17 miles (28 km)
- Vaals to Gulpen | 14 miles (23 km)
- Gulpen to Mheer | 16 miles (26 km)
- Mheer to Maastricht Station | 15 miles (24 km)

Highlights
- Views from the seven summits
- Hiking through the ENCI quarry
- A slice of Limburgse *vlaai*, a local pastry, for an energy boost
- Strolling past the vineyards of South Limburg

Sleep and shelter
Each stage of the DMT ends in a village where you can put your tent up at a local campsite or book a hotel or B&B.

MORE MULTI-DAY HIKES IN
THE NETHERLANDS

Pieterpad | 311 miles (501 km)
This is the Netherlands' most popular trail, mapped in the '70s and '80s by two keen hikers. It goes from the Wadden Sea to Sint-Pietersberg near Maastricht. Expect crowds.

Trekvogelpad | 257 miles (414 km)
This route, the Migratory Bird Trail, stretches from Bergen aan Zee to Enschede. It passes through nature reserves rich in birdlife, especially during migration season.

Krijtlandpad | 56 miles (90 km)
A regional loop translated as Chalk Country Trail, through South Limburg's hills and borderlands with Belgium. Marked with red and yellow stripes, it begins and ends in Maastricht.

07 BELGIUM

ENTRE LESSE ET LOMME

Wild camping in the Belgian Ardennes

In the woods of the Belgian Ardennes, you can hike for days carrying everything you need on your back – food, water, a tent – and barely see another soul. One of the best places to do this is in Libin, home to the 'green' Entre Lesse et Lomme trail, named after the rivers Lesse and Lomme. It's a hike through forested hills, with designated bivouac sites spaced roughly 15 miles (25 km) apart. After a long day on the trail, you can warm up your meal, sit by the fire with fellow hikers, and fall asleep content, ready to do it all again the next day.

48 MILES (78 KM) | 3 STAGES | MODERATE | 3,940 FEET (1200 M)↑

It's early March when my photographer friend Jochem and I decide to tackle our first trail of the season. The sun is finally making a return, and we're ready to stretch our legs. And where better than in the vast forests of the Ardennes, where we can also train on some elevation for upcoming hikes later this year? At around 7pm, we reach the tiny village of Lesse, park by the trail, and get our bearings.

The car park is pitch dark, and for a moment, we wonder if it's even safe. But we grab our headlamps and set off. The trail to the La Virée à Chêne bivouac site is wide and easy to follow, a welcome relief in the eerie stillness of the woods at night. As we near our destination, we spot the warm glow of a campfire.

We're not alone after all, and after a quick chat with Mats, Laurent, and David, some hikers from France who've already been walking for two days, we pitch our tent. It's still cold at night, close to freezing, and I'm grateful for our thick sleeping bags. The sun is warm during the day, but at night, winter hasn't quite let go.

After a restless night, mostly from the cold, we wake up early. Today's stage is the longest, nearly 19 miles (30 km) to the next bivouac site. We quickly pack up the tent, grateful that the sunlight is filtering through the trees, as our hands are freezing handling the gear. With full packs on our backs, we head into the woods near Lesse where the trail leads toward the Lomme River, winding along a wide path covered in leaves. Fortunately, most of the mud has dried up, making the walk much more comfortable.

Since there are no restaurants or shops along the trail, we must carry all our food with us. Carrying three days' worth of water would have been impossible, so we bring a filter to drink safely from the rivers we pass. We collect water from the river, squeeze it through the filter and drink it straight away. Water is easy to find here, with streams and rivers often crossing our path. After seven hours of hiking, we arrive at the Biolin bivouac, a peaceful spot with two round shelters and picnic tables. A few other tents have already been set up, and we swap a few stories with the other hikers and settle in for the evening.

The next morning, after a better night's sleep and slightly warmer temperatures, we pack up, eat breakfast and hit the trail again. My legs feel heavy at first – clearly, I'm out of practice carrying a full pack. But after a few miles, I find my rhythm again. The route is peaceful, and we only see a few foresters and a lone local out for a stroll. After 15 miles (25 km) we arrive at Bané, our final bivouac site. It's a grassy, fenced area with trees, a fire pit and even a compost toilet – a surprisingly welcome luxury. We put our tent up and reunite with the same group from earlier nights. It's comforting to see familiar faces, and although the wood is too damp for a fire tonight, we gather at the pit with our freeze-dried dinners.

By day three, we've really found our groove. Our backpacks also feel lighter now that we've eaten most of our food. The final stage is another 15 miles (26 km), completing the loop. What started as a grey day soon brightens into sunshine as we walk along forest paths tracing the Lomme River back to Lesse. After 48 miles (78 km), we reach the car park. I spot our car and give Jochem a high five. The trail was tougher in places than we expected, but it feels great to be moving again. Spending three days hiking through quiet forests, camping under the stars, and carrying everything on our back is a rewarding and unforgettable way to reset.

07 BELGIUM
ENTRE LESSE ET LOMME

Know before you go

There are no shops, restaurants or accommodation on this trail so you'll need to carry all of your own food, drink and sleeping gear. A tent, sleeping mat and sleeping bag are essential. You can refill water along the way, but you'll need a water filter or purification tablets to make it drinkable. Bivouac sites must be reserved in advance at rando-lesse-lomme.be. Hunting season runs from October to December, and hikers are advised not to walk the trail during that time.

PRACTICAL INFO

Country: Belgium
Start and end point: Lesse
Distance: 48 miles (78 km)
Duration: 3 days
Difficulty: Moderate
Best time to go: March to September
Terrain: Forest, hills
Elevation gain: 3,940 feet (1200 m)

Our suggested stages
- La Virée à Chêne to Biolin | 17 miles (27 km)
- Biolin to Bané | 15 miles (24 km)
- Bané to La Virée à Chêne | 15 miles (25 km)

Highlights
- Sleeping under the stars at designated bivouac sites
- Enjoying the vast forests of the Ardennes
- Experiencing three days of self-sufficiency in nature

Sleep and shelter
This is a bivouac trek, so you'll need to bring all your own camping gear. At each site, you'll find a small flat field, sometimes with wooden picnic tables and a campfire area.

MORE MULTI-DAY HIKES IN BELGIUM

National Park Trail | 68 miles (110 km)
Hike a loop through the National Parc Hoge Kempen, passing sand dunes, open moors, and quiet forest trails.

GR Flemish Ardennes | 98 miles (157 km)
This GR (Grande Randonnée) trail takes you through the beech forests, valleys, and rolling hills of the Flemish Ardennes.

Venntrilogy | 68 miles (109 km)
Walk from the three-border point of Belgium, Germany and the Netherlands to Bütgenbach, passing heathland, forests, castles and old estates along the way.

 LUXEMBOURG

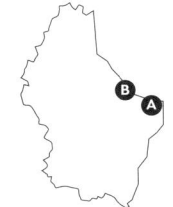

MULLERTHAL TRAIL

Winding through Little Switzerland

Luxembourg's Mullerthal region, often called Little Switzerland because of its towering sandstone rock formations that feel almost alpine, is home to one of Europe's most beautiful hiking networks. From the historic towns of Echternach, Beaufort, and Berdorf, three circular routes cover about 70 miles (112 km) of wooded trails dotted with dramatic rock formations, crevices, and gorges. Winding past castles and rivers, the Mullerthal Trail reveals a Luxembourg that feels far larger and more majestic than its small size on the map suggests.

70 MILES (112 KM) | 6 STAGES | EASY | 7,218 FEET (2200 M) ↑

This long-distance hike is a bit different from others in this book. It consists of three interconnected loops, each about 24 miles (38 km) long, with some overlapping sections. Most hikers choose to base themselves in one town and explore the highlights of each loop as day trips. Thanks to Luxembourg's excellent (and free!) public transport, it's easy to return to your accommodation every evening.

I chose to walk parts of loops 2 and 3 over two days, and tackled loop 1 in one go. Just for the challenge, let's say. There's something special about the Mullerthal, though I can't quite put my finger on it. Maybe it's because I come back each spring, just as hiking season begins. The fresh green woods give me space to breathe, and they stir a sense of freedom and excitement in me for the summer adventures still to come. It's the perfect place to slow down, unwind, and reset. From the Martbusch campsite in Berdorf, where I stay in a pod, I set off on the second loop. The trail heads straight into the forest toward Echternach, Luxembourg's oldest city, before curving back to Berdorf. It's early April and the flowers are beginning to bloom, with the rocks carpeted in a layer of green moss. After two hours of walking, I reach the town centre and pause to explore, stopping for coffee and a pastry from the local bakery.

Back on the trail, I continue towards Berdorf. It's a surprising stretch, passing through Wollefsschlucht, a narrow gorge with sandstone cliffs that soar up to 165 feet (50 m). Stone steps wind through tight passages where the layered rock is clearly visible. I peer down a crevice and see a graveyard of fallen boulders, shrouded in dark moss, likely undisturbed for centuries.

A little further along, I enter the labyrinth: a maze of rock corridors and crevices that defines the region. In early spring, with the trees still bare and the sun hanging low in the sky, the place has an eerie stillness. After a few hundred metres, I leave the maze behind and follow a peaceful forest path back to the campsite, having covered around 12 miles (20 km).

The next day, I walk part of loop 3 from Berdorf to Beaufort, once again starting directly from the campsite (a real luxury). The trail runs alongside a river, and the sun beats down. All is quiet. The path leads through the tiny village of Mullerthal, then on to Beaufort, where the ruins of a large medieval castle immediately catch my eye. Though crumbling, it's easy to imagine its former grandeur. A final stretch through the woods brings me back to Berdorf.

Day three is about testing my endurance: completing an entire loop in a single day. Having already walked parts of loops 2 and 3, only loop 1 remains. The trail begins in Echternach and winds through several small hamlets. I set off early and, for hours, see no one. This loop feels different, with more open farmland and built-up areas. Eventually, I re-enter the forest and pass the trail's most famous rock formations, reaching the finish in just under nine hours at Echternach Abbey. Founded by the Anglo-Saxon monk Willibrord, the abbey was once the heart of a small principality. Even during Roman times, Echternach was a place of significance.

After three days of hiking, I feel calm, almost like a different person. The quiet trails offer space to reflect and disconnect. I head home recharged and grateful.

08 LUXEMBOURG
MULLERTHAL TRAIL

Know before you go

The Mullerthal Trail is ideal for first-time long-distance hikers and is best tackled between April and October. It's a quiet region, perfect for disconnecting and recharging in nature. Winters can bring snow and cold, so plan accordingly. In addition to the three main loops, several extra day circuits offer opportunities to extend your journey. More information is available at hiking-trails.com/trail/mullerthal-trail.

PRACTICAL INFO

Country: Luxembourg
Start and end point: Echternach - Berdorf - Beaufort
Distance: 70 miles (112 km)
Duration: 5 days
Difficulty: Easy
Best time to go: April to October
Terrain: Forest, hills
Elevation gain: 7,218 feet (2200 m)

The three loops
- Loop 1: Echternach - Rosport - Moersdorf - Herborn | 22 miles (36 km)
- Loop 2: Echternach - Berdorf - Mullerthal - Hersberg - Scheidgen | 22 miles (38 km)
- Loop 3: Mullerthal - Blumenthal - Larochette - Beaufort | 24 miles (38 km)

If you'd like to walk all three loops of the Mullerthal Trail as a continuous long-distance hike, follow these suggested stages:

- Echternach to Moersdorf | 11 miles (18 km)
- Moersdorf to Echternach | 12 miles (20 km)
- Echternach to Mullerthal | 7 miles (12 km)
- Mullerthal to Larochette | 11 miles 17 km)
- Larochette Mullerthal | 12 miles (20 km)
- Mullerthal to Echternach | 15 miles (25 km)

Highlights
- The rock labyrinth between Echternach and Berdorf
- Castle ruins at Beaufort
- Sleeping in a camping pod
- Narrow crevices and dramatic cliffs near Berdorf

Sleep and shelter
Campsites and other accommodation are widely available. Many hikers choose a base and use public transport (which is free and frequent) to reach each loop's starting point.

MORE (MULTI-DAY) HIKES IN LUXEMBOURG

Lee Trail | 34 miles (54 km)
This hilly route runs through the Eislek region and follows the Sûre River, with 6,500 feet of elevation gain across three stages.

Minett Trail | 56 miles (90 km)
This trail explores Luxembourg's industrial south, now a UNESCO Biosphere Reserve, where old iron mines have slowly given way to forests and wildlife.

Eislek Trail | 65 miles (105 km)
Cross the Ardennes from Belgium into Luxembourg over five forested stages. This trail links up with the Lee Trail as part of the Escapardenne route.

09 POLAND

MAIN BESKID TRAIL

A quiet trail through the Carpathians

Text: Shanna Bussink

With dense forests, quiet paths, and old mountain huts, the Main Beskid Trail is a dream for anyone who loves both mountains and woods. Stretching for 310 miles (500 km) from Poland's western border with the Czech Republic to its eastern edge near Ukraine, it holds the title of the country's longest marked hiking route, winding through the wild and scenic Beskid Mountains.

310 MILES (500 KM) | 21-26 STAGES | DIFFICULT | 72,120 FEET (22000 M)↑

The trail itself has a rich history. The western section, from Ustroń to Krynica, was completed in 1929, with the eastern part added in 1935. Originally, the trail extended into the Chornohora mountains, which were then part of Poland but are now in Ukraine. Over the decades, this land has seen wars, uprisings, shifting borders, and changing regimes. Even recent milestones like the fall of communism in 1989, Poland joining NATO in 1999, and the EU in 2004 have left their mark. You can feel the history with every step you take.

The route passes through four national parks and crosses six mountain ranges. The highest point, Babia Góra, rises to 5,660 feet (1725 m), which may not sound too dramatic at first but don't be fooled: this is a trail of steep climbs, rocky descents, and plenty of challenging stretches.

As soon as I leave the village of Ustroń, the climb begins. Heading east towards the wildest part of the trail, the route from Chyrowa to Wołosate joins the long-distance European trail E8. It's well marked with red and white signs, making it easy to follow (most of the time).

The first ascent rewards me with sweeping views over Ustroń and, far off, into the Czech Republic. It's September, and this year's *złoty wrzesień*, the golden Polish September, is living up to its name. With the summer holidays behind us, the trail is quiet, and I often don't see another person for hours.

I make my way through forests and over rocky paths. Beskid Śląski is the first mountain area I cross. Here, mountain huts, a ski resort, and war memorials dot the landscape. The trail skirts close to the Czech and Slovak borders before climbing to the summit of Barania Góra. This western section is the highest stretch of the trail and includes Babia Góra, the highest peak overall. Locals call Babia Góra *Matka Niepogód*, the "mother of bad weather." Luckily for me, the skies are clear. It's a Saturday, though, and I'm far from alone. It seems this part of the climb is a popular weekend outing.

From Babiogórski National Park, I continue east into Gorczański National Park. The Gorce Mountains are smaller but no less beautiful. Wildflower-filled fields and endless views make this a particularly beautiful section. After about 105 miles (170 km) on the trail, I reach Turbacz, which at 4,300 feet (1310 m) is the highest point in the area. Both the summit and the nearby hut

are rich in history, as both anti-Nazi and anti-Soviet resistance fighters hid here during the 1940s. Today, the mountain hut houses a small museum dedicated to mountain tourism and culture. Later, I climb Lubań (4,020 feet or 1225 m), where a wooden lookout tower offers views of the Tatras on a clear day without the crowds the Tatras usually attract in summer.

Next, I move into the Beskid Sądecki range, famed for its distinctive flysch rock formations. Here, I spend the night at the Hala Łabowska hut, a place fully dedicated to the Main Beskid Trail. Inside, a detailed trail map and elevation profile are painted on the wall, and each year, an annual celebration is held for the trail.

The following day, I walk down through thick forest to Krynica-Zdrój, one of Poland's most famous spa towns, where locals and visitors line up to drink the mineral-rich waters from public fountains. The fresh mountain air, pure water, and natural springs have made this spot a wellness haven for centuries.

The mood shifts as I enter the Beskid Niski, or Lower Beskids. The name might suggest gentler terrain, but there are still plenty of ups and downs here. This section feels quieter, more remote, and far less developed. Huts are scarce, and warning signs remind hikers we're now in bear country. Rain begins to fall as I reach Magura National Park, the mist only adding to the forest's slightly eerie feeling.

Rymanów-Zdrój and Iwonicz-Zdrój feel like scenes from a film set, with their brightly coloured wooden houses all beautifully preserved. I walk past long stretches of farmland, through forest and fields, before eventually reaching the village of Komańcza with its old wooden church. A curious moment in history took place here. In 1919, there was an attempt by local villagers to unite with other villages that belonged to the Lemko ethnic group and create an independent microstate. But the experiment only lasted three months before the Polish government regained control.

The trail now curves into the Eastern Carpathians, passing lakes that were formed by landslides more than a hundred years ago. The forests here are ancient, and as I enter the Bieszczady Mountains, the ridges grow sharper and the views more striking. This is Poland's third-largest national park and a UNESCO World Heritage Site, making it a fitting end to the Main Beskid Trail.

At the top of Mount Smerek a cross marks 100 years of Polish independence and just a little further on, I pass the freshly renovated Chatka Puchatka hut, named after Winnie the Pooh for its remote, fairytale setting. It's as peaceful and hidden away as the Hundred Acre Wood itself.

From here, the Tatras come into view: the highest peaks in the Carpathians. The Beskids, which form the northern edge of the range, lie mostly in Poland, though parts stretch into Slovakia, the Czech Republic and Ukraine. On some sections, I even walk right along the border. The Carpathians, especially the Beskids, are home to some of Europe's last great primeval forests, which is why the region is often called the Forest Carpathians. These ancient woods are also home to the continent's largest populations of brown bears, wolves, and lynx.

Finally, I reach the far southeastern corner of Poland, still high in the hills and soaking up the views, before descending into the quiet village of Wołosate. The final stretch of the Main Beskid Trail, which follows the ridge line of the Western Bieszczady, is nothing short of spectacular. I couldn't have asked for a better ending.

09 POLAND
MAIN BESKID TRAIL

Know before you go
In Polish, the Main Beskid Trail is called *Główny Szlak Beskidzki*, or GSB for short. It's good to know this in case someone asks if you're hiking the GSB, which is the common name for the route. You won't see many long-distance hikers, but some parts of the trail can get busy with day hikers, especially on weekends. Mobile signal is available most of the way, but it's a good idea to download the Ratunek app before you go. Choose the Góry (mountains) option. This English-language app connects you directly to Polish mountain and water rescue services in an emergency.

You can also earn medals for hiking this trail. The Polish tourism organisation PTTK offers stamp booklets, which you can get at tourist offices and some mountain huts. Collect stamps from huts and landmarks like viewing towers. Each one earns you points, and a certain number of points gets you a bronze, silver, or gold medal. Hike the full trail in 21 days, and you'll earn a diamond medal.

PRACTICAL INFO

Country: Poland
Start and end point: Ustroń to Wołosate
Distance: 310 miles (500 km)
Duration: 21-26 days
Difficulty: Difficult
Best time to go: May to September
Terrain: Mountains, forest, fields
Elevation gain: 72,170 feet (22000 m)

Our suggested stages
The longest stage for a 21-day schedule is 20 miles. The shortest is 10 miles. You can find all of the stages for this trail at hiking-trails.com/trail/main-beskid-trail.

Highlights
- *Pierogi ruskie*, a regional dumpling dish
- *Oscypek*, a traditional mountain cheese, often made from goat's milk
- Homemade schnapps served in the mountain huts

Sleep and shelter
You can stay in mountain huts or villages along the trail. On the western side, there are plenty of options. On the eastern side, huts are less frequent, but accommodation is available in nearby villages. Camping is allowed at most huts and in some basic wild camping spots along the route.

MORE MULTI-DAY HIKES IN SOUTHERN POLAND

Little Beskid Trail | 85 miles (137 km)
Just north of the Main Beskid Trail is the Mały Szlak Beskidzki, a gentle 5 to 6-day trek through the forest that's perfect if you're new to hiking.

The Loop - The Great Beskiden Round | 155 miles (250 km)
A circular hut-to-hut hike through the Silesian Beskids. The route passes villages with hotels and well-maintained huts. Parts of it overlap with the Main Beskid Trail, including the summit of Babia Góra.

Sudeten Main Route | 273 miles (440 km)
Poland's second-longest trail crosses the Crown of Polish Mountains. You'll see waterfalls, rock mazes, lookout towers, and places like the gold mine in Złoty Stok and the fortress at Srebrna Góra.

 GERMANY

SCHLUCHTENSTEIG

Hiking the Black Forest Grand Canyon

This hike feels like stepping into another world. In Germany's Black Forest, the Schluchtensteig trail winds through dense woodland and narrow gorges, and past quiet monasteries where you can also spend the night. And because the trail hugs the Swiss border, you'll even catch a glimpse of the Alps in the distance.

74 MILES (119 KM) | 5 STAGES | MODERATE | 1,080 FEET (3290 M)↑

Our hike begins in the town of Stühlingen, in Baden-Württemberg. Our guesthouse smells faintly of old oak furniture and dated chequered curtains hang in the windows. Schnitzel and potato salad are on the menu tonight: the perfect fuel for the 74 miles (119 km) ahead. The Schluchtensteig is one of Germany's official Top Trails, known for great views and good signage. We're excited to see if it lives up to its name.

From our hotel, we walk straight onto the first stage where wide gravel roads soon turn into narrow forest paths. It's late September, usually chilly in these parts, but the sun peeks through the trees, and the weather is just right. Still, the trail is steeper than we expected. "Germany's not that hilly, right?" we'd thought. But the Buchberg quickly proves us wrong.

Occasionally, we pass a local on the trail who greets us kindly and stops for a chat. At the summit, the literal and figurative high point of the trail, we spot a lone birdwatcher scanning the valley below. We follow his gaze and see the village where we'll end the day. Nearly 19 miles later (30 km), we arrive in Ewattingen, where we spend the night in the only guesthouse in town.

The next day, the trail leads us through the Wutachschlucht, the longest gorge in the area. It's damp and shadowy, and we have to watch our step to avoid slipping on wet rocks and tree roots. Our trekking poles come in handy here. We follow the river through the gorge, the so-called 'Grand Canyon of the Black Forest,' with rock walls rising high beside us. There's no one around. Apart from birdsong and the occasional rustle, it's completely silent. We reach Wutachmühle, an old sawmill, then continue on to Lenzkirch, where we check in for the night.

The guesthouses on this trail are great: solid food, warm beds, no fuss. On day three, we're back on the trail climbing again, this time up the Bildstein, which tops out at 3,720 feet (1134 m). From the summit, we look out over the Schluchsee, a wide reservoir below. A bit further on is the Unterkrummenhof, a traditional restaurant by the lake. The menu is a little on the heavy side (think meat and cheese fondue), and with miles still ahead, we stick to a cold Coke and a bowl of soup on the terrace. Gravel roads lead us into St. Blasien by evening. It's livelier than the other towns, and the huge abbey dominates the view along the Alb River.

Built in the 9th century, it's one of the largest domed churches in Europe; impossible to miss.

The next few stages are more relaxed. You pass through a village each night, so the rhythm settles into a morning climb followed by an afternoon descent. The stretch to Todtmoos is no exception, though the views begin to open up. Dense forest finally gives way to sweeping scenes, and on clear days, you can see the Swiss Alps in the distance. The trail keeps surprising us. After a final stretch through another gorge, we reach Todtmoos, where we spot a bakery that claims, on its door, to be one of Germany's best. We take it at its word and order a slice of Black Forest gateau – rich, chocolatey, and layered with cherries.

By the last day, we've climbed over 10,000 feet (3000 m) and now spend most of our time descending. The trail to the village of Wehr leads through the Wehraschlucht and doesn't bore us for a moment. Every day here has felt different. We chat with a few other hikers, swapping stories and future plans. One thing is clear: this won't be our last time in the Black Forest. After 74 miles (119 km), we arrive in Wehr, a former textile town, and finally put our feet up, ready to rest after a demanding but unforgettable week.

10 GERMANY
SCHLUCHTENSTEIG

Know before you go

The Schluchtensteig is a great choice for newer long-distance hikers or anyone looking for a quiet, week-long adventure. The route is well-marked and not overly technical, with amenities in villages along the way. You'll likely meet other hikers but still enjoy solitude between stops. Bring good rain gear, as the weather in the Black Forest can change quickly. Book accommodation ahead of time, as options are limited in some villages.

The Black Forest is Germany's largest forested region, home to over 1,200 plant and tree species. It's a low mountain range in the country's south-west, bordering France and Switzerland. With more than 14,900 miles (24,000 km) of hiking trails, it's a true paradise for walkers.

PRACTICAL INFO

Country: Germany
Start and end point: Stühlingen to Wehr
Distance: 74 miles (119 km)
Duration: 5-7 days
Difficulty: Moderate
Best time to go: May to September
Terrain: Forest, hills
Elevation gain: 1,080 feet (3290 m)

Our suggested stages
- Stühlingen to Ewattingen | 16 miles (26 km)
- Ewattingen to Lenzkirch | 16 miles (26 km)
- Lenzkirch to St. Blasien | 15 miles (25 km)
- St. Blasien to Todtmoos | 12 miles (20 km)
- Todtmoos to Wehr | 14 miles (22 km)

You can also walk the Schluchtensteig in 6 or 7 days. Check out the stages at hiking-trails.com/trail/schluchtensteig.

Highlights
- A hefty slice of Black Forest gateau
- *Flammkuchen*, a thin, crispy flatbread popular in Germany, at the Schattenmühle
- Tasting the region's famous Black Forest ham
- *Rothaus* beer and local schnapps

Sleep and shelter
You'll find guesthouses (*Gasthäuser*) along the trail, but book ahead, especially during peak season, as availability is limited in some areas.

MORE MULTI-DAY HIKES IN GERMANY

Westweg | 177 miles (285 km)
One of Germany's oldest trails, this route cuts across the Black Forest. Choose between the easier eastern variant or the tougher western route, which includes the Feldberg summit.

Eifelsteig | 194 miles (313 km)
Walk from Aachen to Trier over 15 stages. This trail explores the Eifel, with its volcanic rock formations, forests, and great views.

Malerweg | 72 miles (116 km)
This route through Saxon Switzerland passes dramatic rock formations and panoramic viewpoints. Named the Malerweg, or Painter's Way, it inspired many 19th-century Romantic artists.

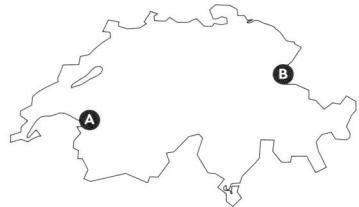

VIA ALPINA 1

250 miles on foot across Switzerland

The Via Alpina 1 is a 250-mile (400 km) trek that crosses Switzerland from east to west, a route that tests your physical and mental stamina. Most days involve climbing more than 3,250 feet (1000 m), but the reward is worth it: jagged peaks, sapphire lakes, wildflower meadows, and cosy mountain huts. The trail is well-marked and connects one village to the next, making it easy to sink into the rhythm of Swiss mountain life. Evenings are spent refuelling with hearty meals and, occasionally, a cheese fondue.

242 MILES (400 KM) | 20 STAGES | DIFFICULT | 77,100 FEET (23500 M)↑

The journey begins in Gaflei, a quiet mountain village in Liechtenstein. At the trailhead, a wooden sign simply reads: *Montreux, 250 miles*. Seeing it sends a shiver down my spine – not out of fear, but from anticipation. That heady mix of uncertainty and excitement. We take our first steps downhill towards Vaduz, the tiny capital, passing beneath the royal Vaduz Castle, where Prince Hans-Adam II still lives. Soon, we cross the Rhine and step into Switzerland. Now the adventure can truly begin.

The Heidiland region, in the canton of St. Gallen, is our first true taste of Swiss trail life. On day two, we enter the peaceful Weisstannen Valley, where green slopes are dotted with dairy cows. Welcome to the land of cheese fondue. But the terrain soon toughens. Crossing into the canton of Glarus, we tackle the first of fourteen mountain passes.

At Foo Pass, a sudden storm rolls in: a less-than-ideal welcome. We shelter with another hiker in a tiny, abandoned hut, waiting patiently for the sun to return. When it does, we follow a breathtaking ridge down to the village of Elm. That evening, in a simple but friendly ski hut above the village, our hosts serve us a massive pot of pasta. We finish almost all of it, so we're relieved when a second pan arrives. We clearly weren't the only hungry ones.

By day four, we've settled into our rhythm, and our legs are feeling stronger. We climb to the car-free village of Braunwald, then descend into the canton of Uri, winding through a fairytale valley flanked by pine-covered slopes. In the quiet hamlet of Urnerboden, we rest for a moment before facing one of the biggest challenges yet: the 6,500-foot (2000 m) climb to Altdorf. Coffee and chocolate fuel us over the Klausen Pass, and twelve hours later, we drag ourselves into Berggasthaus Brüsti, where the kind hostess immediately senses our exhaustion and offers us a cold beer. We feel eternally grateful.

As we head west, the peaks rise dramatically. After a night in Engelberg, an outdoor hub popular with cyclists and hikers, we stay at the striking Hotel Engstlenalp, right beside Lake Engstlensee. Its pink façade and green shutters look like something straight out of a Wes Anderson film.

We're now officially in the Bernese Highlands, the crown jewel of the Swiss Alps. Over several days, we pass the iconic villages of Grindelwald, Lauterbrunnen, and Mürren, hiking alongside the peaks of the Eiger, Mönch, and Jungfrau. The toughest section, known as the 'King Stage,' is also the most beautiful. It ends at the Blümlisalphütte, a high mountain refuge sitting at 9,320 feet (2840 m), beside a glacier. Surrounded by alpine giants, I feel tiny and utterly in awe. Inside the hut, hikers from around the world share tables, food, and stories. Cabin life makes us equals. We get up early the next morning to watch the sunrise, then begin the descent to the turquoise waters of Lake Oeschinen, soaking in the moment as we reach Kandersteg.

HOTEL ENGSTLENALP

Two weeks in, we continue through the stunning highlands toward the French-German language border. From Bunderchrinde Pass, on the way to Adelboden, we spot a bearded vulture: Europe's largest bird, with a wingspan of over 8 feet (2,4 m). It's a rare and unforgettable sight.

The terrain eases as we reach luxurious Gstaad, popular with celebrities. Arriving in dusty clothes, we feel more than a little out of place, but find shelter in a surprisingly affordable youth hostel. The next day, we cross the language border into the canton of Vaud and immediately sense the cultural shift. The food changes, as does architecture; even the mentality seems a little different. Time feels less urgent here in the French-speaking side, and we match the slower pace. We've been on the trail for seventeen days now, and the end is drawing near.

On our last night, something wonderful awaits us. Taking the advice of a fellow hiker, we head to a restaurant at the train station near the summit of Rochers de Naye. It wasn't clear if they had beds, but a quick call secures us a spot. From our position above Lake Geneva, we watch our final sunset, a breathtaking close to an epic adventure.

The next morning, we descend into Montreux, a city famous for its musical history. On the lakeside promenade, beside the statue of Freddie Mercury with his fist raised in triumph, we feel just like him: proud, invincible, fulfilled.

After twenty days on the trail, our time on the Via Alpina was unforgettable – not just for the spectacular scenery, but for the shared encounters, the joy of walking, and the enduring beauty of the Swiss Alps.

11 SWITZERLAND
VIA ALPINA 1

Know before you go

The Via Alpina 1 is a demanding alpine hike, with much of the route above the tree line and nearly every stage crossing a mountain pass. While the trail isn't too technical, it requires fitness. Prepare with plenty of backpack training and be ready for rapidly changing mountain weather.

Stages 10 to 15 of the Via Alpina are also known as the *Bärentrek*, or bear trek. If you don't have time for the full route, this section is a fantastic alternative. It winds through the Jungfrau region, passing glaciers and alpine lakes. In total, the hike involves around 26,900 feet of elevation gain, so be ready to feel the burn!

PRACTICAL INFO

Country: Switzerland
Start and end point: Gaflei (Liechtenstein) to Montreux
Distance: 250 miles (400 km)
Duration: 20 days
Difficulty: Difficult
Best time to go: June to September
Terrain: Mountains
Elevation gain: 77,100 feet (23500 m)

Our suggested stages

- Gaflei (Liechtenstein) to Sargans | 17 miles (28 km)
- Sargans to Weisstannen | 8 miles (13 km)
- Weisstannen to Elm | 14 miles (22 km)
- Elm to Linthal | 15 miles (25 km)
- Linthal to Urnerboden | 10 miles (16 km)
- Urnerboden to Altdorf | 17 miles (27 km)
- Altdorf to Engelberg | 17 miles (29 km)
- Engelberg to Engstlenalp | 7 miles (12 km)
- Engstlenalp to Meiringen | 14 miles (22 km)
- Meiringen to Grindelwald | 14 miles (23 km)
- Grindelwald to Lauterbrunnen | 12 miles (20 km)
- Lauterbrunnen to Griesalp | 14 miles (22 km)
- Griesalp to Kandersteg | 11 miles (17 km)
- Kandersteg to Adelboden | 10 miles (16 km)
- Adelboden to Lenk | 7 miles (14 km)
- Lenk to Gstaad | 14 miles (22 km)
- Gstaad to L'Etivaz | 10 miles (16 km)
  L'Etivaz to Rossinière | 7 miles (14 km)
- Rossinière to Rochers de Naye | 12 miles (19 km)
- Rochers de Naye to Montreux | 8 miles (13 km)

These are the official stages of the Via Alpina 1. Sometimes we stayed in a mountain hut, which is often just a little further than the actual end point of the stage. Check out hiking-trails.com/trail/via-alpina-1 for a specific description of the mountain huts on the trail.

Highlights

- Staying in the Blümlisalphütte
- Cheese fondue by candlelight
- Watching the sunrise over the peaks
- Hiking along the turquoise Lake Oeschinensee

Sleep and shelter

Each stage ends in a village with mountain hotels, or you may pass a hut where you can stay the night. This is a popular trail, especially in summer, so book ahead.

MORE MULTI-DAY HIKES IN SWITZERLAND

Jura Crest Trail | 200 miles (320 km)
Switzerland's oldest long-distance trail stretches from Zurich to Lake Geneva through the Jura mountains. Expect gentle climbs and views of the Black Forest and the Alps.

Bernina Trek | 77 miles (124 km)
A scenic, high-altitude journey. Explore the high mountains of Graubünden while staying in cosy huts run by the Swiss Alpine Association.

Vier-Quellen-Weg | 50 miles (81 km)
A loop through the Gotthard Massif, leading to the sources of four major rivers: the Rhine, Reuss, Ticino and Rhone. Known for its biodiversity and mountain landscapes.

12 FRANCE

GR5 – SAVOIE MONT BLANC

At the foot of Mont Blanc

The GR5 is the crown jewel of Europe's long-distance hiking trails—a red-and-white marked route stretching for 1,430 miles (2300 km) from Hoek of Holland in the Netherlands all the way to the Mediterranean coast in Nice. On our trip we're only tackling a small section, but it's a mighty one: from Lake Geneva to Chamonix, winding through the Savoie Mont Blanc region of France and skirting the edge of the Mont Blanc massif.

62 MILES (100 KM) | 6 STAGES | DIFFICULT | 21,982 FEET (6700 M)↑

Our adventure begins in the small alpine village of Thollon-les-Mémises, just below Lake Geneva. Some hikers start at Saint-Gingolph on the lake's shore, but that means a much longer forest climb. We choose a gentler start, taking the cable car up to about 5,000 feet (1500 m). It's seriously windy, and as we ascend towards Pic Boré at 6,500 feet (2000 m), I grip my trekking poles tightly just to stay upright. The peak itself juts out at an angle, giving it a wild, off-kilter look. I don't hang around long, dropping quickly onto a lower path where the wind finally eases.

Later, we briefly leave the main trail, drawn by the sight of a mountain hut. Dent d'Oche sits just below a jagged summit and looks as if it's been carved straight into the rock. The trail there is steep, with iron cables helping us conquer the climb. At the top, we're rewarded with sweeping views across Lake Geneva and mountain after mountain stretching endlessly into the distance. We rejoin the GR5 on the descent, ready for what comes next.

As we near our first overnight stop – the mountain huts are known here as "refuges" – we find ourselves walking with unexpected company: a family of ibex. Calm and unbothered, they graze quietly just a few feet from the trail, allowing us to pass without a fuss. Refuge de Bise lies deep in a valley, and to our surprise, it's far more comfortable than we imagined. There's a hot shower, rooms that feel almost like a hotel, and a large table where we gather with fellow hikers. Dinner is a hearty three-course affair: soup and fresh bread, followed by a generous plate of potatoes with sausage (or cheese) and beans, and finally, a crème brûlée topped off with a selection of local cheeses. We laugh, swap stories, and soak up the warmth of the communal atmosphere with about twenty other hikers before retreating to our sleeping bags, fully sated.

The next morning brings bad news: thunderstorms are rolling in. As rain and hail begin to fall, it quickly becomes clear that continuing to the next hut isn't safe. We change plans and head down to the village of La Chapelle-d'Abondance instead. After managing to call ahead and cancel our hut reservation, we race the storm. Just before the skies fully open, we arrive at a warm, dry hotel, grateful that we built some flexibility into our itinerary. Safety, after all, comes first.

The rain continues the following day, though the thunder has passed. We hike uphill to Refuge de Trébentaz, the hut we missed yesterday. We warm ourselves by the stove, attempt to dry our soaked gear, then press onwards. It's a long day, and we have miles to make up. The trail hugs the mountainside, shrouded in fog, lending everything an otherworldly feel.

At the next mountain pass, the trail opens up. Rain returns, but the wider path offers space to think. We duck into a mountain café for shelter, where the air is thick with the scent of damp jackets, hot food, and woodsmoke. Sitting by the fire with a Nutella crêpe, we recharge before continuing towards the next refuge, Refuge de Chésery, just over the border in Switzerland. We arrive soaked but satisfied, ready to rest.

Day four brings us back into France, climbing steadily towards Refuge du Folly. The skies finally clear, revealing peaks covered in fresh snow, like someone scattered powdered sugar across them. The final ascent is steep but absolutely worth it. The wooden hut leans into the mountainside as if it has always been there. Inside, we're welcomed by a warm-hearted Nepalese sherpa who works here during the high season. The refuge is bustling, and dinner is a comforting Nepalese curry followed by a shot of *génépi*, a potent local herbal liqueur made from alpine wormwood. Strong stuff!

From here, the trail descends to the famous ski village of Samoëns. We're closing in on the giant now: Mont Blanc. After five days of hiking, the colossal, snow-capped peak finally looms ahead. At 15,771 feet (4807 m), it's the highest summit in the Alps and yet somehow, it feels even larger and impressive than its height suggests.

The next day proves the toughest yet. The trail climbs sharply toward Refuge d'Anterne Alfred Wills, a welcome rest stop. Shortly after, we pass the stunning Lac d'Anterne, which is so blue and picture-perfect, it almost doesn't seem real. One final climb leads us to Refuge de Moëde Anterne. Behind the hut, Mont Blanc dominates the horizon. As evening falls, the sky lights up in a pink sunset, and we pause to soak in the magic of the moment.

On our final day, one last climb awaits. We follow a rocky trail up to Le Brévent, where the cable car waits to ferry us down into Chamonix. One last close-up glance at Mont Blanc, and then it's down to the lively town below. Chamonix buzzes with energy: hikers, alpinists, and outdoor lovers fill the streets, hopping from one outdoor gear shop to the next. It feels like the perfect ending to our journey.

12 FRANCE
GR5 – SAVOIE MONT BLANC

Know before you go

The GR5 runs along well-marked trails through the Alps, passing through small villages and mountain huts. There are lots of intersecting paths, so having a map or hiking app is helpful. The weather changes quickly up here, so check the forecast every day and bring good rain gear. If you're going in July or August, book your hut spots early: they get busy fast.

PRACTICAL INFO

Country: France
Start and end point: Thollon les Mémimes to Chamonix
Distance: 62 miles (100 km)
Duration: 6 days
Difficulty: Difficult
Best time to go: July to September
Terrain: Mountains
Elevation gain: 21,982 feet (6700 m)

Our suggested stages

- Thollon les Mémimes to Refuge de Bise | 9 miles (14 km)
- Refuge de Bise to Refuge Trébentaz | 8 miles (13 km)
- Refuge Trébentaz to Refuge de Chésery | 8 miles (13 km)
- Refuge de Chésery to Refuge du Folly | 14 miles (23 km)
- Refuge du Folly to Refuge de Moëde Anterne | 17 miles (27 km)
- Refuge de Moëde Anterne to Chamonix | 8 miles (13 km)

Highlights
- Sunset over Mont Blanc
- Cheese boards in La Chapelle-d'Abondance
- Lakeside breaks at Lac d'Anterne
- Sipping *génépi* schnapps in cosy mountain huts

Sleep and shelter
You'll find a mix of mountain huts and small hotels in villages along the trail. If weather changes your schedule, it's easy to adjust your plans and stay in nearby accommodation (but book huts ahead, especially in peak season).

MORE MULTI-DAY HIKES IN FRANCE

Grande Traversée des Alpes (GTA) | 385 miles (620 km)
This legendary trail from Lake Geneva to the Mediterranean is the southern section of the GR5 and one of France's most iconic thru-hikes.

GR20 Corsica | 112 miles (180 km)
One of Europe's most demanding trails, the GR20 crosses the craggy ridges of Corsica. Hike from hut to hut or camp along the way for a rugged adventure.

Tour du Beaufortain | 61 miles (98 km)
A scenic loop past alpine lakes and mountain huts, with constant views of Mont Blanc. A quieter alternative to the busy Tour du Mont Blanc.

LIECHTENSTEIN TRAIL

A slow journey through a tiny country

Sandwiched between the soaring Swiss and Austrian Alps, Liechtenstein is a tiny principality with a curious charm. I've always found it a bit mysterious — everyone's heard of it, but few can say why. At just 28 miles (45 km) long, it's the sixth smallest country in the world. But don't let its size fool you: Liechtenstein is full of surprises. The royal family still lives in a castle overlooking the capital, Vaduz. And then there's the Liechtenstein Trail, a 45-mile (75 km) route that zigzags through every municipality, covering almost twice the country's length.

47 MILES (75 KM) | 3 STAGES | VERY EASY | 6,560 FEET (2000 M)↑

It's the perfect way to experience everything Liechtenstein has to offer. The trail winds through the scenic Rhine Valley, past castles and forests, villages and hills, all set against a dramatic alpine backdrop. For our adventure, we base ourselves at the Swiss Youth Hostel in Schaan-Vaduz, an ideal home base for daily explorations. Each morning, we set out to discover a new stretch of the trail, returning in the evening. No heavy backpacks, no strict schedule: just an easy adventure through this lesser-known principality.

We start the Liechtenstein Trail in Schaanwald, in the northeast, right on the border with Austria. You can also walk it in the other direction, and it's worth noting that the trail is accessible all year round, even in winter. A local bus drops us off, and we walk uphill into the forest, passing an old smuggling route near Mauren. At a village bakery, we stop for coffee and a sandwich before continuing towards the Robert Ritter mountain hut, then out onto open farmland. A tractor ploughs the fields ahead, trailed by at least a dozen storks picking through the freshly turned soil. It's a clear day, and the Appenzeller Alps already rise in the distance. After 15 miles (25 km), we reach Ruggell, the northernmost tip of the country.

The next day, we're back in Ruggell and back on the trail. This section winds through sleepy villages; we pass a few locals tending their gardens, but see no other hikers. The climb up to Planken is steeper than expected, the narrow path tangled with roots and requiring real effort. At the top, we rest on a wooden bench and take in the view across the Rhine Valley to the Swiss mountains. You're never truly in the high mountains here, but they're always close, always in sight.

After a short, steep descent, we stop in Eschen for snacks (a Snickers bar, my favourite, and a handful of nuts), then carry on past a white church with a tall red steeple. By late afternoon, we're back in Schaan, our final stop for the day.

The final leg starts strong. From Schaan, we walk into the capital, Vaduz. The streets are neat, lined with museums and high-end boutiques, with a few historic buildings dotted among them. Above it all sits Vaduz Castle, the country's most famous landmark and still home to its prince. It's under scaffolding, but it's still impressive. A steep climb behind the castle brings us to a lookout point, where we pause to trace our route across the country. We tick off the villages we've already passed, before continuing to the ruins of Schalun Castle and gazing out over the Rhine Valley.

From there, the trail climbs to Triesenberg, the highest village in Liechtenstein. The final stretch leads to Gutenberg Castle, which looks like something out of a fairytale: perched on a hilltop, framed by vineyards. Roman roads once passed through here, now it's hikers. A few more miles, and we reach the end of the trail at the Swiss border.

13 LIECHTENSTEIN
LIECHTENSTEIN TRAIL

Know before you go

The Liechtenstein Trail can be walked year-round on well-marked paths. You can either walk the entire route from a single base or book accommodations in the villages you pass through. The official language is German, though various dialects are spoken. Liechtenstein is a constitutional monarchy made up of 11 municipalities. The head of state is Prince Hans-Adam II von Liechtenstein.

PRACTICAL INFO

Country: Liechtenstein
Start and end point: Schaanwald to Balzers
Distance: 47 miles (75 km)
Duration: 3 days
Difficulty: Very easy
Best time to go: All year round
Terrain: Hills, urban, forest
Elevation gain: 6,560 feet (2000 m)

Our suggested stages
- Schaanwald to Ruggell | 13 miles (21 km)
- Ruggell to Schaan | 13 miles (21 km)
- Schaan to Balzers | 20 miles (32 km)

Highlights
- Panoramic views of the Rhine Valley from Planken
- Passing by Vaduz Castle, the royal residence
- Strolling through vineyards near Gutenberg Castle

Sleep and shelter

Use the Swiss Youth Hostel as a convenient basecamp or book hotels and guesthouses in the villages along the route. Accommodation is limited, so it's a good idea to book in advance.

MORE (MULTI-DAY) HIKES IN LIECHTENSTEIN

Fürstensteig | 7 miles (12 km)
A challenging day hike along narrow ledges and steep mountainsides. Take a break at the scenic Gafadura Hut, run by the local alpine association.

Route 66 | 27 miles (44 km)
The toughest multi-day trail in the country, this high-alpine route passes through several mountain huts and showcases Liechtenstein's rugged terrain.

Malbun Loop | 4 miles (7 km)
A short two-hour hike around the mountain village of Malbun, offering constant views of peaks and valleys.

14 ITALY

DOLOMITES UNESCO GEOTRAIL

Walking through time in the Italian Alps

Travel 350 million years back in time on the Dolomites World Heritage Geotrail. These jagged limestone peaks were once coral reefs at the bottom of a tropical ocean, now they rise above one of the most dramatic landscapes in Europe. With a network of traditional and modern mountain huts in some truly spectacular locations, plus plates of hearty South Tyrolean food at the end of each day, it's easy to fall in love with the region.

109 MILES (176 KM) | 10 STAGES | DIFFICULT | 26,247 FEET (8000 M)↑

The full trail stretches 109 miles (176 km) and begins at the Geoparc Bletterbach. It's a fitting starting point and also where you can grab a helmet for the first stage, which involves a short scramble through the gorge itself. We descend into the canyon, picking our way around boulders as red rock walls rise up around us, layered with millions of years of geological history. The Weisshorn looms ahead. At 7,598 feet (2316 m), it's our first major

summit. After climbing through pine forests and alpine meadows, we reach the top, take in the views over South Tyrol, and rest our legs. It's a tough climb, but worth it. Then it's down again, heading for our first overnight stop at Hotel Schwarzhorn, where we drop off the helmets and rest after a solid first day on the trail.

Our next stop is the emerald-green Karersee, a picture-perfect lake framed by dark pine forests and jagged peaks. It's breathtaking but also busy, so we don't linger too long. From there, we continue into Naturpark Schlern-Rosengarten, one of four nature parks along the route.

On day three, heavy rain is forecasted. After just an hour on the trail, we take shelter at Paolina Hütte. The storm hits fast: one of the worst in decades, the hut staff tell us. We change our plans and decide to stay the night. Throughout the afternoon, more soaked hikers arrive.

With the storm behind us, we carry on. The trail grows more demanding: at times we're scrambling over rocky terrain, gripping steel cables bolted into the mountain for balance. We cross several high passes on the way to our next hut. It's sweaty, steady work, and while a good level of fitness helps, it's more manageable than it appears. The passes seem distant at first, but as we focus on each step, they draw closer.

On day four, we reach one of the region's more luxurious mountain huts: the Tierser Alpl Hütte. We spot its distinctive red roof and large skylights from a distance, framed by the towering wall of rock behind it. It's a striking sight. Inside, we're welcomed into a minimalist wooden dining room with floor-to-ceiling windows that have sweeping views of the surrounding mountains. Behind the bar, a tray of freshly baked Linzertorte waits for hungry hikers.

STORMS IN THE MOUNTAINS

Hiking in the mountains often brings unexpected challenges. During our trek in the Dolomites, we were caught in what turned out to be one of the heaviest storms in decades. It threw our plans off completely. We'd pre-booked all our huts, so falling behind schedule wasn't ideal, but in the mountains safety always comes first.

That day, we managed just an hour on the trail before taking refuge in the nearest hut. It turned out to be the right call. The route ahead included steep, narrow paths that would've been treacherous in the rain. As the day wore on, more hikers trickled in, soaked, and we all passed the time with board games and shared stories. In the end, it was a day we hadn't planned, but one we'll always remember. The kind of twist that makes an adventure truly memorable.

That evening, we're treated to a South Tyrolean feast. Not the typical mountaineer's fare, but a carefully prepared three-course meal paired with local Lagrein wine. The pesto pasta, made with regional ingredients, is particularly good. It's the perfect reward after several demanding days on the trail, and we head to bed full and content.

By day five, we're deeper into the Dolomites, crossing into Puez-Odle Nature Park, where the landscape shifts once again. The mountains here look almost sculpted, as if stacked piece by piece. We follow a wide plateau trail from hut to hut, staying high above the valleys at over 6,500 feet (2000 m). Marmots call out from the rocks as birds of prey glide overhead. It's a gentle, panoramic walk along the mountainside, leading us east towards Fanes-Sennes Nature Park.

As we continue, the unique geology of this UNESCO World Heritage Site becomes even more evident. The limestone here is delicate and easily eroded. We see it clearly near Plätzwiese, where a field of fallen red rock fans out beneath a towering peak. Throughout the day, we notice small clouds of dust rising as new debris tumbles down. Even the smallest rockfalls are a reminder not to linger too long. We keep moving and eventually stop for a delicious bowl of pasta and a strong coffee at the next hut. Fuel for the final stretch.

The trail builds to its apex in the final days: the approach to Tre Cime di Lavaredo, or Drei Zinnen, is one of the most iconic places in the Alps. The three peaks, rising side by side like a family, are just mesmerising. We spend the night nearby at the cosy Dreizinnenhütte. It's busy during the day with day visitors, but by evening the hut quietens, leaving just the overnight hikers to soak it all in. As the sun dips, we notice flashes of light high up on the cliffs. There are some hikers sleeping on portaledges, tiny hammocks suspended from the rock face. We watch them in awe.

The next morning, we wake up early to catch the sunrise. As the first red light spills over the Drei Zinnen, I get goosebumps. It's magical. Total stillness, the mountains glowing. For a while, it feels like we have it all to ourselves. It's the perfect send-off before the final stretch to Sexten.

On our last day, we meet two men from the local mountaineering association. They're checking the trail, with wooden posts and tools strapped to their backs, replacing signs and making repairs. At the tiny Büllelejochhütte, we share one last espresso. Then comes one final detour to the Zigmondyhütte where we stand, reluctant to leave. We don't want the walk to end, and as we begin our descent to Sexten, the trail's end point, we already feel nostalgic for South Tyrol.

14 ITALY
DOLOMITES UNESCO GEOTRAIL

Know before you go
The Dolomites in northeastern Italy are among the world's most beloved mountain ranges, known for excellent views and fantastic cuisine. Book your mountain huts well in advance, especially in high season, to secure a bed. Always carry enough food and water, check the weather daily, and bring proper rain gear. A sheet sleeping bag is also required for most huts.

Despite being in Italy, South Tyrol feels very Austrian. After WWI, Tyrol was split in two, leaving the southern half part of Italy. Today, South Tyrol is a mix of Italian flair and Austrian alpine charm, which is reflected in everything from food to signage.

PRACTICAL INFO

Country: Italy
Start and end point: Bletterbach to Sexten
Distance: 109 miles (176 km)
Duration: 10 days
Difficulty: Difficult
Best time to go: July to September
Terrain: Mountains
Elevation gain: 26,247 feet (8000 m)

Our suggested stages
- Bletterbach to Lavazèjoch | 8 miles (12 km)
- Lavazèjoch to Karerpass | 12 miles (20 km)
- Karepass to Tierser Alpl Hütte | 10 miles (16 km)
- Tierser Alpl Hütte to St. Ulrich | 11 miles* (17 km*)
- St. Ulrich to Puez Hütte | 14 miles (23 km)
- Puez Hütte to Armentarola | 13 miles (21 km)
- Armentarola to Sennes Hütte | 11 miles (17 km)
- Sennes Hütte to Plätzwiese | 12 miles (19 km)
- Plätzwiese to Dreizinnenhütte | 10 miles (16 km)
- Dreizinnenhütte to Sexten | 10 miles (16 km)

*You can also choose to spend the night at the Brogles Hütte, 7 miles (11 km) from St. Ulrich.

Highlights
- Sunrise over the Drei Zinnen
- Local dishes like cheese dumplings, *Schlutzkrapfen* (stuffed pasta) and *Schüttelbrot* (a local flatbread)
- Tasting the local wine, Lagrein
- Sleeping in the Tierser Alpl Hütte

Sleep and shelter
Overnight stays are usually in mountain huts along the trail. In some areas, particularly passes or villages without huts, you'll find comfortable mountain hotels as alternatives.

MORE MULTI-DAY HIKES IN ITALY

Ortler High Mountain Trail | 74 miles (119 km)
A challenging trek around the Ortler Massif, also known as the Ortler Höhenweg, with overnights in huts and one stage that crosses a glacier. Ideal for experienced hikers.

Salento Trail | 72 miles (115 km)
A coastal trail in the heel of Italy's boot, this hike winds along narrow beaches and cliffs. Best enjoyed in spring when wildflowers line the path.

Via Degli Dei | 81 miles (130 km)
This "Way of the Gods" pilgrimage from Bologna to Florence passes through rolling hills, ancient towns, and historic monasteries.

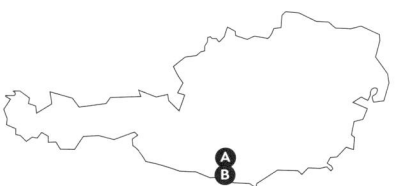

ALPE ADRIA TRAIL

Through Austria's lake country

The Alpe Adria Trail is an incredible long-distance hike stretching for 466 miles (750 km) from the foot of Austria's highest peak, the Grossglockner, all the way down to Muggia, a small Italian port on the Adriatic Sea. Most people take it bit by bit, often doing just one stage a year. We choose a section through Austria's lake-rich province of Carinthia, passing the beautiful lakes of Ossiacher See, Wörthersee, and Faaker See.

62 MILES (100 KM) | 5 STAGES | MODERATE | 8,202 FEET (2500 M)↑

The trail is designed to be accessible: no tough alpine climbs here, just peaceful, well-marked paths linking the Alps with the Adriatic. Since it winds through dozens of handpicked villages, you can easily join wherever it suits you. We started in Arriach, a charming village above Villach near the Slovenian border, which also happens to be the geographic heart of Carinthia.

Right after Arriach, the trail moves from pavement to gravel roads, then into narrow mountain paths.

We pass a few old, empty mountain huts with horses grazing nearby and stop for lunch: cheese wraps on a grassy slope. It's the perfect break before a big climb – almost 4,000 feet (1200 m) up to the Gerlitzen Alp, where we spend the night. The terrace is busy with day-trippers who arrive via the cable car, but by evening it's quiet again. Thunderstorms roll dramatically across the distant Karawanken mountains. It's quite the sight.

The next morning, we head downhill toward Ossiach. The trail winds through larch forests and joins the Pfad der Philosophen, or "Philosophers' Path." Along the way, we pass through a free-standing door and stop to read signs featuring quotes from the Chinese philosopher Laozi, among others. Eventually, we reach Steindorf and catch our first glimpse of Lake Ossiach, the first big lake on our hike. By the time we reach the shore, the sun's out and it's warm, so we jump into the cool water and lounge on the grass for a while before checking into a nearby hotel for the night. Dinner comes with views of the lake, and later we wander around the Stift Ossiach monastery, which has been here for over a thousand years, and tonight is beautifully lit up against the darkening sky.

The following day starts with a steep but refreshing climb through the Ossiacher Gorge. It's short but tricky in spots, especially on the mossy stones, so our trekking poles prove useful. Once out of the gorge, the trail flattens and opens up, and soon we spot the deep blue waters of Lake Wörthersee, our destination for the day. This part of the trail follows old Roman roads that once linked important lakeside towns. Finally, we descend to the lakeshore and settle in at Velden, right on the water's edge.

Day four might be our favourite. We stroll along the edge of Lake Wörthersee, passing grand old hotels that look like they've stepped straight out of *The Grand Budapest Hotel*. With faded stone façades and flower-filled balconies, there's an air of mystery about them. After the lake, the trail leads us to the turquoise waters of Faaker See. Then it's back into the forest for a steady climb up to Baumgartnerhöhe, where we pass the ruins of Finkenstein Castle, once surely an imposing fortress. From the top, we're rewarded with sweeping views over the lakes and mountains of Carinthia. The sun sets behind the peaks, turning the sky a bright red. It's the perfect backdrop for our final night on the trail, spent at the mountaintop hotel.

We should be heading down to Villach the next morning, the official end of our journey, but a nearby peak catches our eye and we decide to keep going. It's too soon to finish just yet. We climb towards the summit of Mittagskogel, winding along rocky, narrow paths until we reach the cross at the summit. From up here, Villach seems a million miles away, down below in the valley.

It feels like a fitting end to this part of the Alpe Adria Trail. We head down, breathing in the fresh mountain air, and arrive in Villach's lively town centre. The cafés are bustling, the promenade alive with people, the mountains we just crossed rising in the background. We grab a coffee and toast another great hike.

15 AUSTRIA
ALPE ADRIA TRAIL

Know before you go

The Alpe Adria Trail is perfect for first-time long-distance hikers. While some stages can be physically demanding, the route avoids technical alpine terrain, making it accessible and enjoyable. You'll pass a village every day with places to sleep and eat, so you can hike light. The best time to go is between late spring and early autumn.

Located in southern Austria, the province of Carinthia borders both Slovenia and Italy. The region boasts over 1,200 lakes, including Wörthersee and Millstätter See, and is part of the Hohe Tauern range, the largest mountain range in the Eastern Alps.

PRACTICAL INFO

Country: Austria
Start and end point: Arriach to Villach
Distance: 62 miles (100 km)
Duration: 5 days
Difficulty: Moderate
Best time to go: June to September
Terrain: Mountains, forest
Elevation gain: 8,202 feet (2500 m)

Our suggested stages
- Arriach to Gerlitzen Alpe | 10 miles (16 km)
- Gerlitzen Alpe to Ossiach | 11 miles (17 km)
- Ossiach to Velden am Wörthersee | 11 miles (18 km)
- Velden am Wörthersee to Baumgartnerhöhe | 14 miles (22 km)
- Baumgartnerhöhe to Mittagskogel to Villach | 15 miles (25 km)

Highlights
- Warm *Kaiserschmarrn*, a fluffy pancake, with cranberry jam
- Sleeping on the Baumgartnerhöhe with views of the lake
- A refreshing swim in Lake Ossiach, Wörthersee, or Faaker See
- *Kärntner Nudeln*, Carinthia's take on stuffed pasta

Sleep and shelter
Each stage ends in or passes through a village with guesthouses, B&Bs, or hotels. In some sections, you'll find higher-altitude mountain huts where you can also stay and eat.

MORE MULTI-DAY HIKES IN AUSTRIA

Adlerweg | 262 miles (422 km)
This classic route crosses Tyrol from east to west, where you can often sleep in mountain huts high in the Alps.

Kaiserkrone | 40 miles (65 km)
A five-day loop around the Wilder Kaiser massif, with views of limestone peaks and cosy mountain hut stays.

Gesäuse Runde | 69 miles (111 km)
A week-long loop through Styria's Gesäuse National Park, starting in Admont, home to the world's largest monastic library.

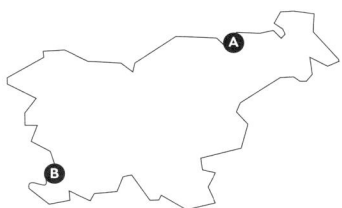

SLOVENIAN MOUNTAIN TRAIL

Crossing Slovenia on foot

Slovenia is home to one of the oldest long-distance mountain trails in Europe: *Slovenska planinska pot*, or Slovenian Mountain Trail (SMT). First established in 1953, it remains one of the greatest routes you can take on foot, and by far the most rugged in this book. Stretching for 383 miles (617 km) and climbing an astonishing 131,000 feet (37,000 m) in total, the trail crosses the country's dramatic alpine terrain. You'll climb as many as 35 peaks, sometimes using your hands more than your feet, and follow the red-and-white Knafelc blazes, named after a famous Slovenian cartographer, each marked with a '1'.

383 MILES (617 KM) | 30-40 STAGES | STRENUOUS | 121,390 FEET (37,000 M)↑

The SMT starts in Maribor, Slovenia's second-largest city. Once part of Austria and later Yugoslavia, Maribor still retains a medieval charm with its red-tiled roofs and cobbled streets. I arrive on a grey morning, a little nervous. At the edge of the city, a sign marks the start of the trail. I snap a quick photo then step into the forest.

The first stage is short, just 8 miles (13 km), and my pace is leisurely. That is, until the distant sound of thunder kicks it up a notch. I'd rather not get soaked or stranded on day one. It's a steep hike from town up to the first mountain hut, Ruška koča, which I reach after three hours, sweaty and wide-eyed. This is it. The start of something I still can't fully grasp.

I've done my research, talked to people, packed well. But still, can I really do this? I still have more than 375 miles (600 km) to go and no idea what to expect. The thought lingers, even as I tuck into a hot meal and fall asleep for eleven solid hours, catching up after a few restless nights of anticipation.

The next few days take me through the Pohorje Hills, the gentlest section of the trail, at least according to the Slovenian Mountain Association's guidebook. Still, I find myself climbing nearly 5,000 (1500 m) feet each day. It's not technical, but it's persistent. I pass quiet huts and sleepy forests, and on day three, I reach Slovenj Gradec, the first town since Maribor. On day four, I meet Robert, an American with a full pack and a helmet strapped to it. We started on the same day but hadn't yet crossed paths. We decide to hike together for a while, which turns out to be a welcome change. These are long days, and it's good to have some company.

On day five, we summit our first serious peak: Raduha. The air is thinner up here, and the views are staggering. But when we descend to the hut we planned to stay at, we discover a problem. It's closed. We'd accidentally booked for the wrong night. It's already dusk, we've been walking for almost eight hours, and the nearest village is still three hours away.

To our enormous relief, a local happens to pass us by and offers to help. After a few phone calls in Slovenian, a man named Rogar picks us up and drives us to his family's holiday farm where we're invited to spend the night. His mother cooks us a warm, hearty Slovenian meal – stuffed peppers – and we get a rare luxury on this trail: a shower. It's a small miracle. A slice of trail magic, no less.

The next day brings something entirely new: a via ferrata. These are alpine climbing routes reinforced with steel cables and iron pegs, originally built during World War I to move troops through the mountains. We ascend into the Kamnik Alps, helmets on, harnesses clipped to the cables. It's steep and technical, but exhilarating. I feel confident, but I can see Robert struggling and I slow down so that we stay together. At the top, he tells me he's heading home. His fear of heights has caught up with him, and there are tougher climbs ahead. It's a wise decision. This trail is no place to push through fear, and safety must always come first. I say goodbye to my new friend, wish him well, and continue alone.

Now eight days in, I reach one of the most technical parts of the trail: narrow paths that skirt cliffs with only the occasional iron cable for support. I arrive at Kranjska koča na Ledinah, a mountain hut where I'll be the only guest that night. Thunderstorms are forecasted, and most hikers have stayed away. Over a simple dinner of jota (a sausage and sauerkraut stew that I'm starting get my fill of on this trip) with the hut wardens, we chat about life in the mountains. They work here from June to October, then head to the valley for winter where they enjoy their

retirement. This is a labour of love for them, and their warmth lifts my spirits.

The next morning, the wardens send me off with a day's worth of food and a slightly modified route. I set out on a short but punishingly steep ascent, more vertical than horizontal, toward a remote mountain bivouac: Bivak pod Skuto. High in the Kamnik Alps, the glass-walled shelter is just magical. Thunder rumbles in the distance as I arrive, just in time. I slip inside, dry and alone.

The following day brings a long, careful descent to the village of Jezersko. The loose gravel and steep drops demand full attention, and I'm relieved when I finally reach the valley. I take a rest day before setting out into the next range: the Karawanks. These trails are easier, and the weather finally smiles on me. I summit Begunjščica and Stol, two beautiful mountains, and for the first time, I feel like I've found my rhythm. To my left: Lake Bled, with its iconic island and castle. Ahead: Triglav, Slovenia's highest peak. To my right: Austria. I'm literally walking on the border. Finally, on day 15, I reach Mojstrana, a charming village at the base of the Julian Alps and prepare for the next stage.

At the foot of the highest mountain, we stare up at a sheer wall of rock. There's no turning back now, and a wide grin spreads across our faces. Surely this is what we came for. I say "we" because yes, by now I'm no longer walking alone. My good friend Chris has joined me for a few days, and just in time. From here, the trail climbs through the highest and most technical peaks, and everything is a little easier with company. You can distract each other, share the weight of difficult decisions, and laugh when the going gets tough.

From the valley, we ascend steeply to Triglavski dom na Kredarici, Slovenia's highest mountain hut, just below the mighty Triglav. The summit is another hour and a half from here. We decide to wait – it's far too crowded in the afternoon – and instead set out at sunrise. At 5am, we climb alone, the world still quiet, the sky beginning to glow. The view from the top stretches endlessly across a magical mountain world. Pure joy.

With thunderstorms forecast again (this seems to be somewhat of a pattern in the Slovenian mountains), we adjust our plan. We'll climb Jalovec, Slovenia's second-highest peak, in the opposite direction. The Slovenians call it the pearl of the Julian Alps, and it's easy to see why. From the cosy hut at Zavetišče pod Špičkom, we prepare for a long, technical day. The trail demands full concentration, and we watch every marking carefully. But

the effort is worth it. From the summit, we gaze out at the mountains before us. Far off in the distance, the snow-covered Grossglockner in Austria glints in the sun.

Then, it's time to part ways. I say goodbye to Chris and thank him for a few unforgettable days. The trail leads me through a final stretch of the Julian Alps and past the beautifully blue Lake Bohinj. I stay here for three nights as storms roll in. It pours and pours, and thunder shakes the sky. But after twenty days, the forced rest is welcome. I sleep deeply and begin to recover. When the skies clear, I cross one last ridge and descend into gentler terrain. The high mountains are behind me. Now, I'm walking toward the coast.
The green hills and easy trails take some getting used to after the sharp climbs of the past weeks. But it feels good to be moving downhill, to feel

the end drawing nearer. I still have a few hundred miles to go, but the shift is real. On social media, I've been in touch with two other hikers: Lara from Belgium and Baethe from Germany. They've been just ahead of me for two weeks but I'm almost catching up. While they take a "zero" (a rest day where, unsurprisingly, you walk zero miles), I arrive, soaked from the rain, at the same hut and finally meet them.

Having decided to walk together for the next few days, we soon pass through Idrija, a charming provincial town, and sleep twice in winter bivouacs. Most huts are closed by mid-September, but many leave a small room unlocked for off-season hikers. It's a joy to share this quiet stretch with others, especially now that we rarely meet anyone else on the trail.

But after a week, it's time to say goodbye again and everyone continues at their own pace. I walk the final leg toward Debeli Rtič, the official endpoint of the Slovenian Mountain Trail. With most huts now closed, finding a place to sleep is sometimes a challenge. After a long 28-mile (45 km) day – and more than a few blisters – I know I'm close. The final steps feel strange: emotional, heavy, surreal. Exactly forty days of walking. Forty days of nature, solitude, encounters, hardship, and awe. Forty days of carving my own path through one of Europe's most beautiful mountain landscapes.

The people I met were kind. The moments, both joyful and hard, were unforgettable. I don't want it to end. But it does. And then, tired and happy, I take a dip in the Adriatic Sea. I will never forget this.

16 SLOVENIA
SLOVENIAN MOUNTAIN TRAIL

Know before you go
The Slovenian Mountain Trail is one of Europe's most demanding long-distance hikes. Trails are steep and often exposed. Some sections require a via ferrata kit, making this trail suitable only for hikers with alpine experience. Slovenians are famously hospitable and happy to chat. Hut hosts may even offer a few too many shots of schnapps! You'll meet few thru-hikers – only around 150 people complete the entire trail each year – so expect solitude, especially in the quieter regions.

Tip: Join the Slovenian Alpine Association or your local mountaineering club to get up to 40% off overnight stays in huts.

PRACTICAL INFO

Country: Slovenia
Start and end point: Maribor to Debeli Rtič
Distance: 383 feet (617 km)
Duration: 30-40 days
Difficulty: Strenuous
Best time to go: June to September
Terrain: Mountains, forest, hills
Elevation gain: 121,390 feet (37000 m)

Our suggested stages
We walked this in 30-40 days. You can find all stages of the trail at hiking-trails.com/trail/slovenian-mountain-trail.

Highlights
- *Struklji*, delicious dumplings stuffed with walnuts
- Climbing Mount Triglav, Slovenia's highest peak
- Staying at a charming vacation farm below Vrn Sjr, run by a young couple who serve only local produce
- Sleeping at Bivak pod Skuto, a stunning bivouac in the Kamnik Alps

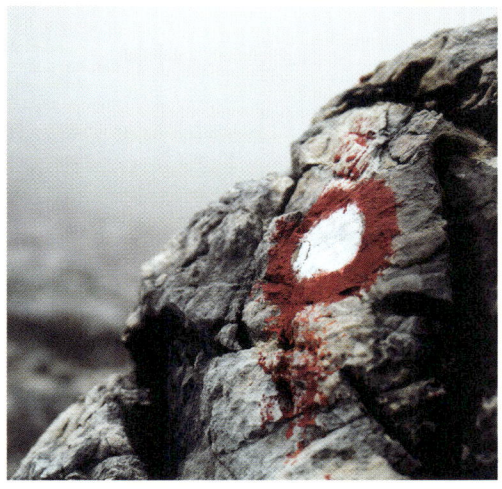

Sleep and shelter
The route passes one or more mountain huts each day, where you can sleep and eat simple but hearty meals. Some stages also go through villages, where you can find hostels, hotels, and B&Bs.

MORE MULTI-DAY HIKES IN SLOVENIA

Juliana Trail | 162 miles (260 km)
A 16-stage loop through Triglav National Park and the Julian Alps, this route follows easy, non-technical trails below the country's highest peaks.

Karavanke Long Distance Trail | 89 miles (143 km)
A one-week trek along the Karawanken range, from Jezersko to Kranjska Gora, with views over Lake Bled, the Sava Valley, and the Julian Alps. Great for beginner hikers.

Koroška Mountain Trail | 143 miles (230 km)
A quiet trail through the Mežica, Drava, and Mislinje valleys. Walk it as a loop or enjoy it in shorter stages.

17 SPAIN

GR121 TALAIA IBILBIDEA

A pilgrimage along the Basque coast

Every year, along Spain's wild northern coast, thousands of pilgrims walk west towards Santiago de Compostela. The region is crisscrossed by a network of hiking trails, with the Camino del Norte being the most famous. But if you stray from the camino, you'll find plenty of GR routes that trace the coastline, head inland, and pass through towns where *pintxos* – the Basque Country's take on tapas – and wine are plentiful.

53 MILES (86 KM) | 4 STAGES | MODERATE | 7,415 FEET (2260 M)↑

We choose to follow the GR121 Talaia Ibilbidea, part of the wider GR network in the Basque Country, but decide to walk east so that we meet the pilgrims going the other way. It just seemed more appealing that way. The road to Santiago can get very crowded, after all, and sometimes you're just walking in one long line.

We start in Ondarroa, a quiet fishing village just an hour from Bilbao, and spend the night in a hotel right above the cliffs, with waves crashing beneath us. The Basque weather is famously unpredictable, but the forecast looks good, so we decide to cover as much ground as possible on day one. As we walk from one bay to the next, the trail climbs quickly, hugging the coastline and offering sweeping views of the Atlantic. Our first stop: coffee and a thick slice of tortilla. Then on to Deba, a picture-perfect

village with whitewashed houses and orange-tiled roofs, tucked away in the green Basque hills. This is technically the end of stage one, but we keep going, eager to press on.

Approaching Zarautz, we follow a narrow path clinging to the cliff's edge, eventually dropping down to the beach. Here we see the famous flysch formations – layered rocks shaped by millions of years of tectonic movement. We pause to take it in. Zarautz is lively, full of surfers and beachgoers, and after a long day, we reward ourselves the Basque way: hopping from bar to bar, sampling pintxos and sipping wine as the sun sets behind the waves.

The next morning, we leave the buzz of Zarautz behind. The trail climbs again, following a rugged path along the sea. Along the way, we pass a rest stop for pilgrims: a small table offering coffee and cake, free to take, with a donation jar for those who want to contribute. We pause for a rest and chat with some of the pilgrims. They're from all over: Swedes, Poles, Brits, Dutch. Many have just started their over-500-mile (800 km) journey to Santiago. Despite the rain, the mood is cheerful, and everyone seems content. We add a few coins to the donation jar and continue on our way, feeling recharged by this pleasant encounter.

San Sebastian, or Donostia in Basque, is the next stop. The provincial capital, with its impressive bay on the Bay of Biscay, is known for its food culture. We check in at the hostel and leave our backpacks before seeking out one of the best pintxos bars, Txepetxa, which has been recommended by every foodie we've spoken to. The anchovies are as good as promised and the beer goes down a treat. Before we know it, the place is packed. Over loud chatter, we watch the Real Sociedad match on the

TV above the bar and make our plan for tomorrow, the final leg.

On the final day, the weather shows its full Basque character: bursts of sun, sudden downpours, and strong gusts of wind whipping across the cliffs. But it doesn't stop us from covering a solid 18 miles (30 km) before taking a tiny ferry across the bay at Pasaia, clinging to the railing and hoping we make it across. From there, the path climbs once more, then weaves through forest and along the coast until, finally, we descend into Hondarribia, the trail's endpoint. Across the water lies France.

Four days. That's all it takes, but it feels like a much longer journey. The wild sea, the rolling green hills, the constant ups and downs from village to cliffside to beach. It never gets dull. And with good food and great trails, the Basque Country more than delivers. What a place to walk.

17 SPAIN
GR121 TALAIA IBILBIDEA

Know before you go
Stretching across northern Spain and southwestern France, the Basque Country is a unique region with a strong sense of identity and culture. The Basques have preserved their ancient language, Euskara, and a proud heritage of independence. The landscape is a mix of green hills and dramatic coastal cliffs along the Bay of Biscay. The food is a highlight: world-famous Basque cuisine features *pintxos*, fresh seafood, meat stews, and artisanal cheeses.

PRACTICAL INFO

Country: Spain
Start and end point: Ondarroa to Hondarribia
Distance: 53 miles (86 km)
Duration: 4 days
Difficulty: Moderate
Best time to go: April to October
Terrain: Coast, hills
Elevation gain: 7,415 feet (2260 m)

Our suggested stages
- Ondarroa to Zumaia | 14 miles (22 km)
- Zumaia to Orio | 10 miles (16 km)
- Orio to San Sebastian | 10 miles (16 km)
- San Sebastian to Hondarribia | 20 miles (32 km)

You can also walk the last leg in two days by staying overnight at Pasai Donibane.

Highlights
- *Pintxos*, small, flavour-packed Basque snacks
- Hiking the dramatic flysch cliffs
- Visiting the market hall in Zarautz for fresh sheep's cheese
- Wandering the lively streets of San Sebastián

Sleep and shelter
Every stage ends in a town or village with plenty of accommodation options. Hostels, hotels, and Airbnbs are widely available.

MORE MULTI-DAY HIKES IN SPAIN

GR11 | 522 miles (840 km)
A spectacular 45-day journey across the Spanish Pyrenees, from the Mediterranean Sea to the Atlantic Ocean.

Camino Primitivo | 200 miles (320 km)
The original pilgrimage route to Santiago de Compostela. You can walk from Oviedo to Santiago in about two weeks.

Carros de Foc | 40 miles (65 km)
A challenging hut-to-hut trek in Aigüestortes National Park in the Catalan Pyrenees. Expect long climbs and nights in mountain huts.

# 18 PORTUGAL

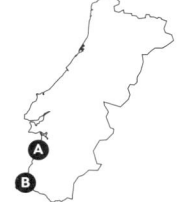

FISHERMEN'S TRAIL

Walking Portugal's wild Atlantic coast

Few trails capture the imagination quite like the Fishermen's Trail. This long-distance hike is often listed among the most beautiful coastal walks in the world by the likes of *Lonely Planet* and *National Geographic*. So, forget Portugal as simply a sun destination and discover the country as a place for walking. The trail winds along a jagged coastline, connecting fishing village after fishing village. It can be tough going, especially when walking on sand, but with the wild Atlantic always by your side, it's pure joy.

141 MILES (227 KM) | 12 STAGES | MODERATE | 8,530 FEET (2600 M)↑

The Fishermen's Trail was the first long-distance hike I ever completed in Europe. That's why, perhaps, it holds a special place in my heart. Cheesy, I know, but still. With many hikes behind me now, I see it as the perfect introduction to multi-day walking. The trail is physically demanding. There's a lot of sand, and with a heavy backpack, it can get tiring – but it's never technically difficult. With the right mindset, I believe anyone can do it. The trail offers so much: culture, food, fellow hikers… A lot of memories to look back on with real fondness.

A bumpy bus ride from Lisbon takes us north to Sines, followed by a short taxi to the trailhead at São Torpes. The first stage immediately throws us into the thick of it. We leave the asphalt behind and my feet sink straight into the sand. It's a real struggle in those first few steps, and, of course, my backpack is once again far too heavy. Luckily, I have my trekking poles, which help ease the strain. The first stage is short – just 6 miles (10 km) – and after around three hours we reach Porto Covo, a small fishing village with the whitewashed houses so typical of Portugal. Off the coast, a few fishermen cast their lines for the evening meal, an apt welcome to the trail. We'll encounter many more scenes like this in the days to come.

After a good night's sleep, stage two is next: 12 miles (20 km), or around eight hours of walking, according to the official trail booklet. I imagine it won't take that long, but I'm wrong. The path runs almost entirely over deep, sandy paths. What a day. For nearly the whole route, we walk along cliffs where the sea crashes below. It's loud but strangely soothing. There's a calming rhythm to the waves. After nearly eight hours, we arrive in Vila Nova de Milfontes, a surfing hotspot with a laid-back vibe. I collapse onto the roof terrace of our hostel, and we toast the day with a cold beer.

After eight hours in the sand, my legs and calves burn. Today's stage is shorter and we head inland, and it stays that way for the next few days. The trail becomes less sandy and far easier to manage. I find myself moving through thick scrub and I'm surprised by the variety in the landscape. In Almograve, after a shorter walking day, we head to the beach for a break and, we hope, a swim. But the sea is too wild, so we settle for paddling. The sun sets slowly as we walk back to the hostel.

We continue towards Zambujeira do Mar and Odeceixe. Now and then, the path crosses the Historical Way, the other long-distance route in the area, which starts in Santiago do Cacém and heads south, further inland. On day five, we walk past bison, zebras and ostriches. A bizarre sight in these parts, but the trail passes by the private zoo of Isabel dos Santos, once said to be Africa's richest woman. The story goes that Dos Santos, daughter of Angola's former president, brought the animals with her to Portugal when she fled the country.

Every day on the Fishermen's Trail, we meet a group of hikers who keep the same pace. Some days we walk together with Alex from Germany, and in the evening, we often eat with the rest of the group. It always makes for great conversations. We meet a couple from England, for example – Lisa and Peter – who discovered hiking when they turned 50. Peter is even planning to take on the Appalachian Trail after this stint in Portugal. Six months across America.

For many, the trail ends on day six in Odeceixe, and we celebrate as a group and bid our new friends farewell. Many hikers, my friend Jochem included, choose to walk only the five original stages. Later, many more stages were added, and I decide to continue walking these on my own.

Having left Alentejo behind, I follow the trail into the Algarve. It now passes cork plantations, wide gravel roads and farmland. I can tell I'm nearing the end. The sea, once to my right, now appears straight ahead. I'm approaching the southwestern-most point of mainland Europe: Cabo de São Vicente. Europeans once believed this was the edge of the world. The trail leads along high cliffs to the 80-foot (24 m) lighthouse built in 1846. Many naval battles have been fought here in the past – British, Spanish, Portuguese and Dutch ships clashing in the waters. Rounding the cape feels like a small victory of my own. From here, just three days remain until Lagos.

First, I walk to Sagres. Surfers float in the water, waiting for the perfect wave, while I take the chance to rest after walking 125 miles (200 km). It's a bit busier here than in Alentejo, but tourists mainly stick to the beaches. This is one of the trail's most stunning sections, but also one of the toughest. The path climbs up and down constantly – cliff to beach, beach to cliff – but the views more than make up for it. From the cliffs, I take in one beautiful cove after another, each gleaming with long stretches of white sand.

From Sagres, I continue to the village of Burgau, where I spend my last night in Casa Grande. It's a true gem. The large house belongs to Sally, an elderly British lady who has decorated it in a traditionally British style. It could almost be a royal residence. After twelve days of walking, I feel weary but happy and sit down for a solid meal. The next morning, after a full English, I set off on the final stretch to Lagos, along soft sandy paths.

This hike has been an unforgettable experience – at times demanding, but always worth it for the scenery and the people. Spending so much time with fellow hikers means you form bonds quickly. After just a few days, it feels like we've known each other for years. You laugh; you share stories. For me, that's what makes hiking so special: the meaningful connections you make along the way.

18 PORTUGAL
FISHERMEN'S TRAIL

Know before you go

The Fishermen's Trail is part of the Rota Vicentina, a large network of hiking routes in southwest Portugal. Alongside this coastal route, the Rota Vicentina also includes the Historical Way, which runs inland from Santiago do Cacém to Cabo de São Vicente. You'll also find several circular day hikes in the region, making it suitable for both long-distance and short-stay walkers. One popular option is to hike the stretch to Odeceixe, which takes five days – perfect for a one-week trip when you include travel time.

PRACTICAL INFO

Country: Portugal
Start and end point: São Torpes to Lagos
Distance: 141 miles (227 km)
Duration: 12 days
Difficulty: Moderate
Best time to go: All year round
Terrain: Coast, hills
Elevation gain: 8,530 feet (2600 m)

Our suggested stages
- S. Torpes to Porto Covo | 6 miles (10 km)
- Porto Covo to Vila Nova de Milfontes | 12 miles (20 km)
- Vila Nova de Milfontes to Almograve | 9 miles (15 km)
- Almograve to Zambujeira do Mar | 14 miles (22 km)
- Zambujeira do Mar to Odeceixe | 12 miles (19 km)
- Odeceixe to Aljezur | 14 miles (23 km)
- Aljezur to Arrifana | 11 miles (17 km)
- Arrifana to Carrapateira | 12 miles (19 km)
- Carrapateira to Villa do Bispo | 12 miles (20 km)
- Villa do Bispo to Sagres | 12 miles (20 km)
- Sagres to Burgau | 15 miles (25 km)
- Burgau to Lagos | 9 miles (15 km)

Highlights
- *Açorda*, a traditional Alentejo herb soup with homemade bread
- A crisp glass of vinho verde, Portugal's "green wine"
- Cosy hiker hostels along the route
- Reaching Cabo de São Vicente, the southwestern-most tip of Europe

Sleep and shelter
You'll find plenty of accommodation in the villages along the trail, from hostels to hotels. Campsites are available, but wild camping isn't permitted as the trail crosses sensitive nature reserves.

MORE MULTI-DAY HIKES IN PORTUGAL

Historical Way | 163 miles (263 km)
The inland counterpart to the Fishermen's Trail. Follow gravel roads past cork plantations and villages from Santiago do Cacém to Cabo de São Vicente.

GR22 - The Great Route of the Historical Villages | 373 miles (600 km)
Visit 12 historic villages and beautiful natural parks, including the UNESCO-listed Douro Natural Park, on a journey through Portuguese heritage.

Via Algarviana (GR13) | 186 miles (300 km)
Hike from the Spanish border across the quiet interior of the Algarve to the Atlantic coast. A lesser-known route through one of Portugal's most famous regions.

How do you tackle a long-distance hike?

Figuring out where to begin can be overwhelming. Some trails capture the imagination, like the Pacific Crest Trail, which runs for 2,650 miles (4265 km) from Mexico to Canada, or New Zealand's Te Araroa, which stretches 1,864 miles (3000 km) across both islands. These so-called 'thru-hikes' where you follow a single trail for weeks or months across a country, are undeniably inspiring and make it onto many people's bucket lists. But they're not always the best place to start.

If you're new to long-distance hiking, it's worth dreaming big but starting small. There are plenty of more manageable trails that are perfect for building confidence and learning the ropes. This book includes 18 of them. They'll help you understand your body, your limits, and what gear you actually need (and what you don't). With a few shorter trails under your belt, those longer routes will feel much more within reach and you'll be far less likely to cut them short, which happens more often than you'd think.

Find your Santiago

Not all trails lead to Santiago, but some of the best ones do. Spain's Camino de Santiago is the world's most walked long-distance trail, with over half a million people completing it each year. For many, it's no longer a religious pilgrimage. The challenge itself is what draws them in. People walk it to reflect, to reset, or to mark a turning point in their lives. Some are searching for clarity after a big change. Others simply want an adventure. But you don't have to walk to Santiago to find all that. Any long-distance hike can be your Santiago. When I found myself at a crossroads, I hiked the Slovenian Mountain Trail. The effort and focus it demanded helped me make decisions, rebuild confidence, and feel grounded again. Reaching the Adriatic Sea at the end felt, to me, like arriving in Santiago de Compostela.

Hike slow, go far

Long-distance hiking isn't a competition. It's not about how many trails you've ticked off or how quickly you finish them. In fact, slowing down might be the best thing you can do. When you take your time, you experience more: more of the landscape, more connection with other hikers, with locals, and even with yourself. You settle into trail life. You move at your own pace, not anyone else's.

Some days, you'll breeze through 20 miles (30 km). Other days, your legs might protest after just a few. That's all part of it. Tomorrow is always a fresh start, so take it slow. You'll go further than you think.

10 TIPS FOR LONG-DISTANCE HIKERS

Getting started can feel overwhelming, so here are ten tips to make your next hike a little easier. Some might seem like common sense, others might be things you haven't thought of yet.

1. **Choose the right trail** The right trail can make all the difference. It means more enjoyment and fewer risks. Think about the length, daily distances, elevation, and difficulty. Consider how remote it is and how often you'll find food, water, or shelter. The more support along the way, the easier your hike will be.

2. **Only pack the essentials** A lighter backpack makes every step easier. Take only what you truly need. There's a packing list on page 260 to help you strike the right balance.

3. **Check the weather daily** It's essential to stay updated, especially in the mountains or on more technical trails. If storms or heavy rain are forecasted, change your plans. Set off early, take a rest day, or adjust your route. Remember, flexibility keeps you safe.

4. **Book in advance** During peak season, popular trails and mountain huts can fill up quickly, especially in places like the Dolomites. Reserve ahead when you can. If your plans change or the weather turns, most places offer free cancellation.

5. **Bring enough water and food** Always carry at least 1.5 litres of water (more if resupply points are rare). Bring salty, high-energy snacks to keep you going; nuts or chocolate bars (I'm partial to a Snickers) both work well.

6. **Start early** Getting on the trail early helps you beat the heat (or afternoon storms) and gives you more time to take breaks, slow down, or just enjoy where you are. In the mountains, mornings are often the most stable time weather-wise.

7. **Be flexible** Even with the best planning, the trail will throw you curveballs. Stay open. Adjust as needed. Trust that things will work out; they usually do!

8. **Start small** Don't jump into a multi-week hike right away. Try a shorter trail first. It gives you the chance to test your gear, see what kind of hiking suits you, and learn what not to pack next time (we've all carried too much at some point).

9. **Train locally** You don't need a gym. Head outside with your full pack. Wear the boots you plan to hike in. Get out in all kinds of weather and try to walk on unpaved trails: that's the best preparation.

10. **Hike slow, go far** This is your hike, not anyone else's. Don't feel pressured to match someone else's pace. Take your time. Go at a rhythm that feels right for you. That's how you'll go the distance.

Find more tips and information on hiking-trails.com

YES, YOU CAN HIKE TOO

"Anyone can hike this trail." I've found myself saying that a lot lately, maybe a little too much. But I believe it. Sure, some of the trails in this book require training, experience, or a bit of technical know-how. But most of them can be walked by anyone.

The hardest part, as with so many things, is just starting. It takes courage, some planning, and a bit of boldness. Sometimes it takes months, even years, to build up to that first step. It did for me. I thought about the Slovenian Mountain Trail for two years before I finally set foot on it. But once I did, everything got easier. My motto: don't overthink it, just go.

Walking is one of the most natural things we do. But in a world where your groceries, takeaways, and shopping are delivered to your doorstep, we sometimes forget that. Taking the time to walk, properly and regularly, is one of the best things you can do for your body and your mind. Even 15 minutes a day has been shown to reduce stress, ease depression, and improve your overall health.

So if a short daily walk can do that, imagine what a long trail might do. I haven't done extensive research, but I *have* done the hikes. And I can say this: long-distance hiking changed my life. It pushed me out of my comfort zone and gave me space to reflect. It helped me see what matters. It made me stronger, more grounded, and it introduced me to some incredible people. It made me appreciate small joys: fresh coffee in the morning, the feeling of sunshine on my face, a simple "hello" from a stranger. Even now, back in everyday life, those little things feel bigger. So here's my advice: try it. Take a walk. Discover a trail. Discover, or rediscover, something about yourself. Or just have the time of your life, and enjoy the ride.

LEAVE NO TRACE

Hiking is one of the most sustainable ways to travel, but every trip still has an impact. That's why it's important to leave as little trace, as light a footprint, as possible. I try to be conscious of this, but I'm not perfect. I've taken flights I could've swapped for trains, and I've probably dropped the occasional wrapper without noticing. The point isn't perfection, it's awareness.

Thankfully, there are plenty of small actions that make a big difference. Some are obvious, others less so. But together, they can help you hike more lightly on the planet. Here are a few easy ways to make your next adventure more sustainable.

Leave No Trace, an organisation dedicated to protecting nature, has outlined seven key principles to help walkers minimise their impact:

1. **Plan ahead and prepare** Being well prepared helps prevent problems and pollution. Bring a bag for your rubbish, for example. If you're camping, plan your route so you stay in designated spots.

2. **Travel and camp on durable surfaces** Pitch your tent on hard or barren ground, not on delicate vegetation. Stick to marked camping areas whenever possible.

3. **Dispose of waste properly** Sort it correctly when you get back to town, and don't leave any rubbish in the mountain huts you visit.

4. **Leave what you find** Don't pick flowers or move any rocks or natural materials. There's a whole ecosystem at work, even if you can't see it.

5. **Minimise campfire impacts** Only light fires in designated spots and only when it's safe. If in doubt, it's best to skip the fire altogether.

6. **Respect wildlife** Don't feed animals, don't chase them, and keep your dog on a lead, especially around cattle.

7. **Be considerate of others** Make way for fellow hikers and step aside on narrow trails.

Not quite off the beaten path
Early on, I didn't give it much thought, but staying on the path really does matter. Straying off trail causes erosion and damages fragile plants. Especially in busy hiking areas, it's important to stick to the marked route. If you pass through a gate, always close it behind you, as farmers rely on those boundaries. And when it comes to wildlife, admire animals from a distance and never feed or disturb them.

Travelling by train
Heading to the start of your hike? Most trails in this book are easily accessible by public transport. It's sustainable, comfortable, and if you book early, often quite affordable. If you're travelling with others, consider sharing a car or combining train and car travel. And if flying is unavoidable, try offsetting your emissions through organisations like Carbon Neutral Britain, Make it Wild, or Forest Carbon, to name just a few. Travel consciously!

Camping responsibly
Putting a tent up always has some impact on the soil and local biodiversity, so try to use designated camping spots whenever possible. If there aren't any, choose a firm surface with little or no vegetation to avoid damaging the area. Don't leave any food scraps or gear behind, and if you move branches or other natural materials, put them back where you found them. Plus, always carry an extra bag for any leftover food or waste.

Why join an alpine club?
If you want to help protect the trails, joining an alpine club is a great choice. The Austrian and German Alpine Associations look after over 24,580 miles (40.000 km) of hiking trails, along with hundreds of mountain huts. They ensure trails remain walkable and huts safe and accessible, whether that means a fresh coat of paint, upgrading the showers, or even relocating a hut to protect the ground beneath. As a bonus, members often receive discounts of up to 40% on hut stays.

Trail difficulty
Each trail in this book has a difficulty rating from very easy to strenuous. The easier routes are suitable for almost everyone; the tougher ones require fitness, experience, or both. Remember, weather can change everything: wind or rain can turn an easy hike into a tough one.

WHAT TO PACK (AND WHAT NOT TO)

For a long-distance hike, you don't need to carry much. In fact, the less you lug around each day, the easier and more enjoyable your hike will be. Of course, you'll still need the essentials, and depending on the trail you choose, you may need to adjust or add gear. You'll find a detailed packing list for each type of trek (hut hike, long-distance trail, or shorter walk) at hiking-trails.com/gear.

Bring along a few non-essentials too – things that make the trip a little more comfortable or enjoyable. For me, that's an electric toothbrush. I know some hikers saw their toothbrushes in half to save on weight, but I'm always glad to have my electric one with me. For you, it might be an e-reader, a journal, headphones, or even a book of extra-difficult sudokus for the long evenings in a hut or tent. Pack light but pack happy.

Essentials
- Hiking shoes
- Backpack with rain cover
- Layered clothing: T-shirts, fleece, down jacket, shorts, long trousers, base layers (merino wool works great), underwear, hiking socks
- Rain gear: waterproof (hardshell) jacket and trousers
- Quick-drying towel
- Trekking poles
- Water (min. 2 litres) and high-energy snacks (nuts, chocolate, cereal bars, wraps)
- Hat, sunglasses, sun cream
- Power bank
- First-aid kit, including a rescue blanket
- Small rubbish bags
- Toiletries: toothbrush, toothpaste, soap, shampoo

Navigation
- GPS watch (optional)
- Map of the area
- Navigation app like Komoot or Outdooractive

Camping gear (for overnight hikes)
- Lightweight tent with footprint (groundsheet)
- Sleeping bag
- Sleeping pad
- Inflatable pillow
- Cooking utensils: burner, pot, spork, lighter
- Freeze-dried meals
- Water filter or purification tablets
- Headlamp
- Pocket knife
- Sitting pad

If you're doing a hut-to-hut hike, consider joining your local alpine or mountaineering club. Your digital membership card (don't forget to download it!) can get you up to 40% off overnight hut stays and helps support trail and hut maintenance in the Alps and Pyrenees.

WHAT HIKING SHOES SHOULD I WEAR?

Hiking shoes come in all shapes and sizes. The most important thing is that they fit well and feel comfortable. No one wants to hike for days with blisters. The best shoe for you depends on the terrain and conditions. A forest trail in Belgium calls for different footwear than a high-alpine trek, for instance. Here's a quick overview of the different types:

Type A: Lightweight, low-cut hiking shoes Great for short or easy walks close to home.

Type B: Lightweight, high-top hiking shoes Supportive boots that protect your ankles and work well for most hut-to-hut hikes.

Type C: Heavy-duty, high-top hiking boots Designed for tough terrain and heavier backpacks. They have stiffer soles and are often crampon-compatible for crossing glaciers.

Type D: Alpine boots Stiff, rugged boots built for technical mountaineering. You won't need these for the trails in this book.

You can choose waterproof boots (often with GORE-TEX membranes) or non-waterproof ones. I only opt for waterproof shoes on wet trails (like in Scotland) or if snow is involved. Most of the time, I prefer non-waterproof boots as they breathe better, keeping your feet cooler and drier overall.

Another option is trail running shoes. Many hikers love them because they're light and comfortable but they offer less ankle support and stability, so they're best suited for experienced hikers or trail runners. If you're new to them, train your ankles with stability exercises and try them out on day hikes before tackling a longer trail.

WHO MADE THIS BOOK?

ELMAR TEEGELBECKERS

Elmar spends months of his time out on the trails. He is often searching for hidden gems in his favourite countries, such as Slovenia, Norway and Switzerland. He's the main writer of this book, but above all a true lover of trails.

When he's not out hiking, he brings hikers together in the Netherlands and abroad through his community on thru-hiking.com and organises various events. He is also the founder of hiking-trails.com, a database of detailed trail descriptions created to inspire hikers for their next adventure. Before that he worked for the Dutch Alpine Association (NKBV), until he lost his heart to long-distance hiking. His motto: Life is better on the trails!

More info on hiking-trails.com and thru-hiking.com.

JOCHEM DE JONG

Outdoor photographer Jochem is happiest in nature, always searching for the perfect picture. In recent years, he has completed more than 25 long-distance trails and documented them for this book. For Jochem, the more challenging the hike, the better. Many of these routes he walked together with Elmar, and alongside his work as a photographer he helps to build the hiking communities on hiking-trails.com and thru-hiking.com.

Epic mountain landscapes and the reward of an ice-cold beer after a long day on the trail are his personal highlights, and whenever possible he loves discovering new places together with his girlfriend.

More info on jochemsfocus.nl

INDEX

PRACTICAL INFORMATION

10 Tips for long-distance hikers 256
Hike Slow, Go Far 254
How do you tackle a long-distance hike? 254
Leave No Trace 258-259
Packing: essentials 260
Preparation 256
Shoes 265
Storms in the mountains 184

18 EUROPESE COUNTRIES

Austria 196-207
Belgium 92-101
Denmark 68-79
England 42-55
France 154-167
Germany 128-139
Italy 180-193
Liechtenstein 168-179
Luxembourg 104-115
Netherlands, The 80-91
Norway 14-29
Poland 116-127
Portugal 238-251
Scotland 30-41
Slovenia 210-225
Spain 229-237
Sweden 56-65
Switzerland 140-151

72 TRAILS

Adlerweg 207
Alpe Adria Trail 197
Archipelago Trail 79

Bernina Trek 151
Beskiden Round, The Loop – The Great -, 127
Bohusleden 65

Camino Primitivo 237
Camøno Trail 69
Carres de Foc 237
Coast to Coast Walk 43

Dolomites UNESCO Geotrail 181
Dutch Mountain Trail 81

Eifelsteig 139
Eislek Trail 115
Entre Lesse et Lomme 93

Finnskogleden Trail 29
Fishermen's Trail 239
Fürstensteig 178

Gesäuse Runde 207
GR Flemish Ardennes 101
GR5 Savoie Mont Blanc 155
GR11 237
GR20 Corsica 167
GR22 – The great route of the historical villages 251
GR121 Talaia Ibilbidea 229
Grande Traversée des Alpes 167
Great Glen Way 41

Hadrian's Wall Path 55
Hærvejen 79
High Coast Trail 65
Historical Way 251

Jotunheimen Traverse 29
Juliana Trail 225
Jura Crest Trail 151

Kaiserkrone 207
Karavanke Long Distance Trail 225
Koroška Mountain Trail 225
Krijtlandpad 91
Kungsleden 65

Lee Trail 115
Liechtenstein Trail 169
Little Beskid Trail 127
Lofoten Crossing 15

Main Beskid Trail 117
Malbun Loop 178
Malerweg 139
Minett Trail 115
Mols Bergje Trail 79
Mullerthal Trail 105

National Park Trail 101

Olavsleden, St. 29
Ortler High Mountain Trail 193

Pennine Way 55
Pieterpad 91

Route-66 178

Salento Trail 193
Schluchtensteig 129
Skåneleden 57
Skye Trail 41
Slovenian Mountain Trail 211
South West Coast Path 55
Speyside Way 41
Sudeten Main Route 127

Tour de Beaufortain 167
Trekvogelpad 91

Venntrilogy 101
Via Algarviana 251
Via Alpina-1 141
Via Degli Dei 193
Vier-Quellen-Weg 151

West Highland Way 31
Westweg 139

SLOW TRAVEL EUROPE — HIKING TRAILS

Slow Travel Europe is a concept by
mo'media publishers

Text & photography
Elmar Teegelbeckers, Jochem de Jong, Shanna Bussink, Chris König, Bart Pawlik and Katie Mitchell

Art direction
Jelle F. Post

Editing
Ezra van Wilgenburg, Katie Mitchell

All rights reserved
No part of this book may be copied, displayed, extracted, reproduced, utilised, stored in a retrieval system or transmitted in any form or by any means, electronic, mechanical or otherwise including but not limited to photocopying, recording, or scanning without the prior written permission of the publisher. No part of this book may be used or reproduced in any manner for the purpose of training artificial intelligence technologies or systems.

Publishers' Note
Every effort has been made to ensure that the information in this book is accurate at the time of going to press. The publisher welcomes any information or suggestions for correction or improvement. Please send us an email at info@momedia.nl.

Authors' Note
Make sure you are well prepared when you go hiking. We explain how to do this on pages 254 to 265. You can find more information on our website, where we share additional routes and useful tips. Make sure to follow us on Instagram @_hiking_trails and don't forget to share your own hikes with us.
More info on hiking-trails.com

Disclaimer
Hiking is an outdoor activity that involves inherent risks. Routes, weather conditions, and terrain can change at any time. You are responsible for your own decisions on the trail. Proper preparation, up-to-date information, suitable equipment, and honest self-assessment are essential. The author and publisher cannot be held liable for accidents, injuries, or losses that may occur while following the routes described in this book.

© 2024, Uitgeverij FJORD
Original title: *Hiking Trails – De mooiste langeafstandswandelingen van Europa*
Text & photography: Elmar Teegelbeckers, Jochem de Jong, Shanna Bussink, Chris König, Bart Pawlik and Peter van der Aa
Art direction: Jelle F. Post

© 2026, English translation, mo'media publishers
Translation: William Simpson, Elmar Teegelbeckers and Katie Mitchell
Art direction: Jelle F. Post

Slow Travel Europe – Hiking Trails
ISBN 978 94 9333 881 4
NUR 500, 502, 512

Slow Travel Europe
Also available in this series: *Platform Europe* (unforgettable train journeys across the continent) and *Going North* (inspiring travel stories from Denmark, Sweden and Norway).

MOMEDIAPUBLISHERS.COM